BEST OF THE BEST

Fast & Fabulous

Soups, Salads
and
Sandwiches

Gwen McKee
and
Barbara Moseley

QUAIL RIDGE PRESS
Preserving America's Food Heritage

Library of Congress Cataloging-in-Publication Data

Best of the best fast and fabulous soups, salads and sandwiches / edited by
   Gwen McKee and Barbara Moseley ; illustrated by Tupper England.
   p. cm.
      Includes index.
      ISBN-13: 978-1-934193-32 7
      ISBN-10: 1-934193-32-1
   1. Soups. 2. Salads. 3. Sandwiches. I. McKee, Gwen. II. Moseley, Barbara.
TX757.B4145 2009
641.8'13--dc22   2009027634

Copyright ©2009 by Quail Ridge Press, Inc.

ISBN-13: 978-1-934193-32-7 • ISBN-10: 1-934193-32-1

On the cover: Mai-Thai Good Shrimp Soup (page 41), Black and Blue Sliders (page 184),
Nutty Cranberry Apple Salad (page 96), and Mousse Shots (page 212)

Photos by Greg Campbell • Food styling by Bobbi Capelli
Text page art by Tupper England • Design by Cynthia Clark
Printed in the United States of America

QUAIL RIDGE PRESS

P. O. Box 123 • Brandon, MS 39043
info@quailridge.com • www.quailridge.com

Contents

Preface 7

SOUPS 9
    Soup Mixes 10
    Vegetable Soups 12
    Meat and Seafood Soups 28
    Bisques 43
    Chowders 46
    Gumbos 54
    Stews 57
    Full color insert follows page 64
    Chilis 65
    Chilled Soups 70

SALADS 73
    Green Salads 74
    Picnic Salads 83
    Fruit and Gelatin Salads 95
    Pasta and Rice Salads 107
    Meat and Seafood Salads 113
    Full color insert follows page 128
    Salad Dressings 133

SANDWICHES 143
    Tea and Brunch Sandwiches 144
    Cold Sandwiches 151
    Hot Sandwiches 157
    Subs and Po-Boys 172
    Wraps and Pockets 177
    Burgers and Dogs 184
    Full color insert follows page 192

SEASONINGS 197

SWEETS 201

Index 213

Gwen McKee and Barbara Moseley

Preface

Barbara Moseley and I have edited and assembled over ninety cookbooks over the years. We continue to search for and create recipes that are easy to make and deliver a tasteful flavor that adds joy to a meal.

With *Fast & Fabulous Soups, Salads and Sandwiches,* we have directed this commitment and goal to three categories of recipes that people enjoy in restaurants, but may need some inspiration and guidance to achieve the same experience in their own kitchen. We believe this cookbook will serve this purpose.

Our soup section contains 112 recipes that range from a thin broth to a full hardy stew. This collection of recipes offers a pleasing first course to the meal, as well as a hearty soup that could be the main meal. We have broadened the soup chapter to include chowders, gumbos, bisques, and stews, and have added ingredients and enhancements that we feel heighten the tastefulness of each recipe.

The 108 recipes in the salad section offer a variety of salads and dressings that will provide an almost endless range of tastes and textures. From the classic Cobb, Waldorf, and Caesar, to salads that are particularly appropriate for a picnic setting, to salads that feature fruit and offer a refreshingly light taste, to salads that contain chicken, ham, beef, pork, or shrimp that will elevate the salad to full meal status . . . we've come a long way from salads that were simply lettuce and tomatoes.

Also included in this section is a wide range of recipes for salad dressings. Some of these 61 recipes are intended for a particular salad . . . others are for salads in general. Each dressing recipe is intended to bring a special spark . . . one that somewhat alters the texture while enhancing the taste.

Sandwiches have come a long way since the Earl of Sandwich wanted his meat put between bread slices so he wouldn't get his fingers greasy, and therefore could continue his gambling while eating his snack. This event supposedly occurred late one night in 1762. Almost 250 years later, the sandwich has become the most convenient and commonly prepared quick meal. We have included a variety of sandwiches from simple lunch box favorites to fancy tea sandwiches, and from wraps and pockets to dogs and burgers.

Then we wanted you to have our best recipes for some popular seasonings that we especially enjoy, including Cajun, Bay, Greek, Taco, Italian, and Salad Supreme.

And for no other reason than I like desserts, we have added a few in a special Sweets chapter, just in case you share my taste for a bite of something sweet.

For those of you who tell us you enjoy reading cookbooks, we added sidebar fun facts, giving added dimension to recipes and preparation, and sometimes just fun stuff to read. Our cookbooks are all about sharing, and we can't wait to share our research of things we have learned and continue to enjoy.

We hope *Fast & Fabulous Soups, Salads and Sandwiches* will bring new enjoyment to your kitchen, and plant some ideas for you to use these recipes as a springboard to an even more spectacular creation of your own. As always, our bottom line is all about taste, taste, and taste!

Gwen McKee

8

Soups

Soup Mixes

Vegetable Soups

Meat and Seafood Soups

Bisques

Chowders

Gumbos

Stews

Chilis

Chilled Soups

Chicken Noodle Veggie Soup Mix

So nice to bring to a friend who needs a boost to make them feel better.

1⅓ cups medium egg noodles, divided
1 teaspoon garlic powder
1 tablespoon chicken bouillon granules
¼ cup red lentils or green split peas
1 (1½-ounce) package dry vegetable soup mix

Layer ingredients in a pint jar: ½ noodles, garlic powder, bouillon, lentils, remaining noodles, then veggie soup mix. (Add more noodles on top if jar is not packed tight.) Attach a card with recipe title and these instructions:

Boil 6 cups water. Add contents of jar; bring back to a boil. Reduce heat and cook 20 minutes.

Editor's Extra: If desired, stir in 1 package frozen stew mix vegetables and diced chicken or turkey with 1–2 more cups water. Cook until vegetables are tender.

At-The-Ready Soup Mix

Just add water! Fun to tie a ribbon around a cellophane bag or jar of this to take to a friend.

3 tablespoons beef bouillon granules
1 cup dried split peas
3 tablespoons dried onion flakes
2 teaspoons dried Italian seasoning
⅔ cup uncooked rice

Mix ingredients and seal in a jar or celophane bag. When ready to make soup, just bring 4 quarts water to a boil, add soup mix, then simmer covered about 45 minutes.

Editor's Extra: If you have leftover ham or ham bone, toss in pot for extra flavor.

2-Mug Tortilla Soup Mix

¼ cup crushed tortilla chips
¼ cup instant rice
1 envelope vegetable soup mix
2 teaspoons chicken bouillon granules
½ teaspoon onion powder
¼ teaspoon garlic powder
¼ teaspoon cumin

Combine all in a bowl; mix well. Half between two zipper bags and place each bag in a gift mug. Attach a tag on each mug with these instructions:

Empty contents of bag into mug. Add 1 cup boiling water. Stir, cover, and let sit for 3 minutes.

Freeze any leftover broth you might have in ice cube trays, then transfer to sealable bags or containers. So nice to perk up not only soups, but all kinds of vegetable and pasta recipes as well.

Potato Soup in a Jar

1¾ cups instant mashed potatoes
1½ cups dried milk or coffee creamer
2 tablespoons instant chicken bouillon
2 teaspoons dried minced onion
1 teaspoon dried parsley
1½ teaspoons Greek seasoning

Combine all ingredients in a 1-quart jar; mix well. On gift tag write:

Add 1 cup boiling water to ½ cup soup mix; stir until smooth.

Editor's Extra: Take ½ cup in a ziploc bag to work or in the car when traveling . . . all you need is a cup of hot water!

Easy Cheesy Veggie Soup

4 teaspoons chicken bouillon granules
Parsley and pepper to taste
1 quart water
1 ($10\frac{3}{4}$-ounce) can cream of chicken soup
1 ($10\frac{3}{4}$-ounce) can cream of mushroom soup
2–3 small potatoes, peeled, cubed
1 (4-ounce) can mushroom pieces, drained
1 (14-ounce) package frozen mirepoix blend
   (chopped onions, celery, carrots)
1 (16-ounce) bag frozen soup vegetables
1 pound Velveeta, cubed

Combine bouillon, parsley, pepper, and water in large soup pot. Add soups and stir till smooth. Add potatoes and mushrooms and continue cooking till potatoes begin to soften. Add frozen vegetables and cook till done. Add Velveeta; stir until melted. Serves 6–8.

Traditional Vegetable-Beef Soup

An all-time favorite.

1 pound round steak, cubed
2 tablespoons oil
1½ cups cubed, peeled potatoes
1½ cups sliced celery
1½ cups sliced carrots
1½ cups chopped onions
2 cups frozen succotash
5½–6 cups water
½ cup mini elbow macaroni
1 teaspoon Italian seasoning
1 ($14\frac{1}{2}$-ounce) can diced tomatoes, undrained

Brown beef in oil in a $4\frac{1}{2}$-quart Dutch oven; add remaining ingredients and bring to a boil. Reduce heat and simmer, covered, 50 minutes. Serves 6–8.

Editor's Extra: Make this easier by subbing 2–3 packages frozen mirepoix blend for the celery, carrots, and onions.

This is the story of stone soup. When a great famine in post-war Europe caused people to jealously hoard their food, a soldier wandered into a village asking for some and was told there wasn't a bite in the whole province. He announced he would therefore make a stone soup to share with them all. From his wagon, he pulled out a caldron, built a fire under it, and filled it with water. He then pulled an ordinary stone out of a velvet pouch, dropped it into the pot, and began to boil it.

The villagers gathered round while he stirred. The soldier licked his lips: "Hmmm, it's good, but stone soup is much tastier with cabbage." Soon a villager brought a cabbage, which the

(continued)

12

Roasted Vegetable Soup

No shortcuts here . . . but the taste is worth it.

2 small red potatoes
1 green bell pepper, halved, seeded
1 medium onion, unpeeled
2 medium tomatoes
1 small acorn squash, halved
3 cloves garlic, unpeeled
1½ cups tomato juice
½ cup water
1 tablespoon oil
1 tablespoon red wine vinegar
¼ teaspoon black pepper

Preheat oven to 400°. Place vegetables on nonstick baking sheet sprayed with cooking spray. Bake 35–40 minutes, but remove garlic and tomatoes after 10 minutes. Remove rest after full time and let stand 15 minutes till cool enough to handle.

Peel vegetables and garlic and chop coarsely. Combine half the chopped vegetables, tomato juice, water, oil, and vinegar in food processor or blender; process until smooth.

Combine vegetable mixture, remaining chopped vegetables and black pepper in large saucepan. Bring to a simmer over medium heat for 5 minutes till heated through. Stir constantly. Top each serving with parsley or cilantro and sour cream, if desired. Serves 4.

(continued)

soldier cut and added to the soup. "Ah, yes! And I think a bit of salt beef would make it fit for a king," he exclaimed. The butcher ran off and managed to find some. And so it went with onions, mushrooms, carrots, potatoes, etc., until there was indeed a grand soup! All the villagers had a feast and learned a good lesson.

The moral of the story is that by working together, a greater good is achieved for all.

Greens, Beans, Carrots, and Things Soup

A vegetarian's delight.

1 ½ cups chopped onions
2 teaspoons minced garlic
½ pound tiny carrots
2 tablespoons oil
1 ½ cups sliced mushrooms
6 cups water or vegetable broth
⅓ cup barley
1 (16-ounce) can Great Northern beans, drained, rinsed
2 bay leaves
1 teaspoon sugar
1 teaspoon dried thyme
7 cups collard greens, washed, stemmed, chopped
1 tablespoon white wine vinegar
¼ teaspoon hot pepper sauce

Cook onions, garlic, and carrots in oil in Dutch oven over medium heat, stirring, 3 minutes. Add mushrooms; cook and stir 5 minutes or till tender.

Add broth, barley, beans, bay leaves, sugar, and thyme. Bring to a boil over high heat. Reduce heat, cover and simmer 5 minutes. Add greens; simmer 10 minutes. Remove bay leaves. Stir in vinegar and pepper sauce. Add salt and pepper, if desired. Serves 8.

18 Karat Gold Italian Soup

2 (14-ounce) packages frozen mirepoix blend
(chopped onions, celery, carrots)
½ medium head cabbage, chopped
2 small zucchini, chopped
2 tablespoons oil
1 (28-ounce) can diced tomatoes with basil, garlic, and oregano, undrained
2 (15-ounce) cans cannellini beans, rinsed, drained
4 cups chicken broth
4 cups tomato juice
1 cup dry red wine or water
Salt and pepper to taste

Cook mirepoix blend, cabbage, and zucchini on medium heat in oil in Dutch oven about 5 minutes, stirring occasionally. Stir in remaining ingredients. Heat to boiling; reduce heat. Cover and simmer 1 hour. Serve with grated Parmesan cheese, if desired. Serves 12.

History tells us that soups, stews, pottages, porridges, gruels . . . all evolved according to local ingredients and tastes. Russian borscht, Italian minestrone, French onion, Chinese won ton, New England chowder, Spanish gazpacho . . . they are all variations on the same theme.

Borscht Made Easy

1 (14½-ounce) can diced tomatoes, undrained
1 (16-ounce) can diced beets, undrained
1 (14½-ounce) can beef broth
2 cups finely shredded cabbage
½ cup instant potato flakes
1 teaspoon sugar
½ teaspoon dried dill weed
½ cup light sour cream
¼ cup sliced green onions

Combine all ingredients except sour cream and green onions. Bring to a boil; reduce heat. Cover and simmer 10–15 minutes. If you prefer a smoother soup, purée mixture. Serve in soup bowls with a dollop of sour cream sprinkled with green onions. Serves 4–6.

sweating onions, leeks, garlic, and celery over low heat before adding liquid will soften them and enhance their flavors.

Tres Bien French Onion Soup

Very good indeed.

2 cups thinly sliced onions
2 tablespoons butter
1 (32-ounce) carton beef broth
1 teaspoon Worcestershire
Dash of pepper
4 slices French bread, toasted
¾ cup shredded Swiss, Gruyère, or mozzarella cheese

Sauté onions in butter in large saucepan over medium-low heat, covered, 8–10 minutes or till tender and golden, stirring occasionally. Stir in beef broth, Worcestershire, and pepper. Bring to a boil; reduce heat. Cover and simmer 10 minutes. Place toasted bread on baking pan; sprinkle with shredded cheese. Place bread under broiler till cheese melts and turns light brown. Ladle soup into bowls and float bread on top, cheese side up. Serves 4.

Easy Roasted Red Pepper Soup

1½ cups frozen chopped onions
2 teaspoons chopped garlic
1 tablespoon olive oil
1 (28-ounce) can crushed tomatoes with basil
1 (12-ounce) jar roasted red bell peppers
2 (14½-ounce) cans chicken broth
1 teaspoon sugar
¼ teaspoon crushed red pepper
¼ teaspoon coarse salt

In 4-quart pot, cook onions and garlic in oil 3 minutes, stirring constantly, till crisp-tender. Add remaining ingredients. Heat to boiling, then simmer 15 minutes. Serves 4–6.

Roasted Corn Soup Topped with Crabmeat

1 (16-ounce) package frozen whole-kernel corn,
   thawed
1–2 tablespoons cooking oil
2 cups chopped onions
1 ½ cups coarsely chopped red bell peppers
4 (14½-ounce) cans chicken broth, divided
½ teaspoon crushed dried thyme
⅛–¼ teaspoon cayenne pepper
⅓ cup all-purpose flour
½ cup light cream
⅔ cup chopped cooked crabmeat

Spread corn in a single layer on a 10x15-inch baking pan with foil, lightly greased. Roast at 450° for 10 minutes; stir. Roast 10 minutes more until golden brown, stirring once or twice. Remove from oven; set aside.

Heat oil in a 6-quart pot. Stir in onions and red peppers and cook over medium heat 3–4 minutes till almost tender. Add roasted corn, 3 cans of broth, thyme, and cayenne pepper. Bring to a boil; reduce heat. Simmer, uncovered, 15 minutes.

In a large screw-top jar, combine remaining can of broth and flour. Cover and shake well; stir into soup. Cook and stir till slightly thickened and bubbly. Stir in cream; heat through. Ladle into bowls and spoon crabmeat on top. Serves 6.

Western Cheese Corn Soup

Big flavor in a bowl.

1 cup chicken broth
1 (16-ounce) package frozen whole-kernel corn,
  thawed, divided
2 tablespoons butter
1 (4-ounce) can diced green chiles
1 teaspoon taco seasoning
1 teaspoon minced garlic
2 cups milk
1 cup chopped cooked chicken
1 ($14\frac{1}{2}$-ounce) can diced tomatoes
1 cup shredded Monterey Jack cheese

Purée broth with half the corn in blender. In a large saucepan, combine purée, butter, remaining corn, chiles, seasoning, and garlic. Bring to a boil; reduce heat. Simmer, uncovered, 10 minutes. Stir in milk, chicken, and tomatoes; heat through. Remove saucepan from heat. Stir in cheese until melted. Serves 6–8.

White Bean Soup

2 green onions, thinly sliced
1 garlic clove, minced
$\frac{1}{2}$ teaspoon dried oregano
2 teaspoons olive oil
1 ($14\frac{1}{2}$-ounce) can vegetable broth
1 (19-ounce) can white beans, rinsed, drained
$1\frac{1}{2}$ teaspoons fresh lemon juice
Coarse salt and ground black pepper to taste
2 tablespoons freshly grated Parmesan

Sauté onions, garlic, and oregano in oil over medium heat until onions are soft, about 3 minutes. Stir in broth and beans; cook until heated through, about 4 minutes. Mash some of the beans against the side of the pot with spoon to thicken soup. Stir in lemon juice; season with salt and pepper. Sprinkle with Parmesan cheese just before serving. Serves 4.

Steamin' John Soup

4 strips uncooked bacon, chopped
1 large onion, chopped
2 garlic cloves, minced
2 (15-ounce) cans black-eyed peas, undrained
1 (14½-ounce) can chicken broth
½ cup water
2–3 tablespoons Tabasco
1 teaspoon dried thyme leaves
1 bay leaf
2 cups cooked rice
2 tablespoons minced fresh parsley

Sauté bacon, onion, and garlic in large saucepan over medium-high heat about 5 minutes or until vegetables are tender. Add peas with liquid, broth, water, Tabasco, thyme, and bay leaf. Bring to a boil. Reduce heat to low; cook, covered, 15–20 minutes, stirring occasionally. Remove and discard bay leaf.

Combine rice and parsley in bowl; spoon rice evenly into 6 serving bowls. Ladle soup over rice. Serves 6.

Cheesy Black Bean Soup

This simple five-ingredient soup is rich with cheese and chunky with corn, black beans, and tomatoes.

1½ cups milk
1 (1-pound) block Mexican Velveeta, cubed
1 (15-ounce) can whole-kernel corn, drained
1 (15-ounce) can black beans, rinsed, drained
1 (14½-ounce) can diced tomatoes, undrained

In large saucepan, combine all ingredients. Cook and stir over medium-low heat until cheese is melted and soup is blended and hot, 7–10 minutes. Serves 4–6.

Soup is generally defined as a liquid savory dish. Other countries call it suppe, zuppa, sop, sopa, sopen. . . . But no matter what you call it, it is a basic dish that is served around the world. Often eaten as an appetizing first course, it can certainly be the main dish, especially when served with hearty breads.

Ever wonder just how popular soup is? Americans sip over 10 billion bowls of soup every single year. That's pretty popular!

Homemade Mushroom Soup

A far cry from the canned variety!

½ onion, thinly sliced
1 teaspoon minced garlic
1 tablespoon butter
1 tablespoon olive oil
8 ounces sliced fresh mushrooms
1 (14½-ounce) can chicken broth
1¼ cups water
¼ cup sherry (optional)
¼ cup tomato paste
½ teaspoon black pepper
¼ cup finely shredded or grated Parmesan cheese
Snipped parsley for garnish

Sauté onion and garlic in butter and oil in a large saucepan over medium heat 5 minutes. Stir in mushrooms; cook, covered, 5 minutes or until mushrooms are tender. Stir in remaining ingredients. Bring to a boil; reduce heat. Simmer, covered, 20 minutes. Top servings with Parmesan cheese and parsley. Serves 4.

Fresh Cream of Mushroom Soup

1 pound fresh mushrooms, chopped
½ stick butter
3 tablespoons all-purpose flour
½ teaspoon each: salt and pepper
1 cup heavy cream
1 (14½-ounce) can chicken broth
1 tablespoon dry sherry (optional)

In large saucepan, sauté mushrooms in butter about 10 minutes, stirring occasionally, until mushrooms are golden brown. Stir in flour, and salt and pepper; cook and stir till thickened. Gradually add cream and broth till hot. Stir in sherry, if desired. Serves 6.

Turkey Mushroom Soup

2 tablespoons butter
2 cups sliced fresh mushrooms
1 (14-ounce) package frozen mirepoix blend
  (chopped onions, celery, carrots)
$4\frac{1}{2}$ cups water
2 tablespoons beef bouillon granules
$\frac{1}{8}$ teaspoon black pepper
$\frac{1}{2}$ cup rice
$1\frac{1}{2}$ cups chopped cooked turkey
2 tablespoons chopped fresh parsley
1 teaspoon chopped fresh thyme

Melt butter over medium heat in a large saucepan. Add mushrooms and mirepoix blend; cook and stir until crisp-tender. Add water, bouillon, and pepper. Bring to a boil; stir in rice. Return to a boil; reduce heat. Simmer, uncovered, 10 minutes. Stir in turkey, parsley, and thyme; heat 10 minutes. Serves 6.

Quick-To-Fix-Peanut Soup

2 tablespoons butter
1 rib celery, finely minced
1 packet dry onion soup mix
1 quart chicken broth
$\frac{1}{2}$ cup creamy peanut butter
1 cup milk or cream
1 tablespoon flour

Stir first 5 ingredients in a saucepan; heat and stir till smooth. Shake milk with flour in a jar, then stir into soup. Garnish with a few crushed peanuts, if desired.

When adding water to a hot pot of soup, it's best to use hot tap water.

21

Take a guess . . . who eats more soup . . . men or women? Typically, women seem to be more than twice as likely to eat soup for lunch than men.

Secret Broccoli Soup

okay, the buttermilk is the secret. And this is good hot or cold.

1 cup chopped onion
6 tablespoons butter, divided
3 (14½-ounce) cans chicken broth
1½ teaspoons Greek seasoning
2 (12-ounce) packages frozen chopped broccoli
⅓ cup flour
1½ cups milk
1½ cups buttermilk
½ pound Velveeta, cubed

Sauté onion in 2 tablespoons butter in Dutch oven. Add broth and seasoning. Bring to a boil; add broccoli; simmer, covered, till tender.

Melt remaining 4 tablespoons butter in medium saucepan over medium heat. Whisk in flour and continue to stir for 1–2 minutes. Whisk in milk and buttermilk; stir till thickened. Add to chicken broth in Dutch oven. Add cubed cheese and continue to stir until very hot and cheese is melted but DO NOT BOIL. Garnish with sour cream, if desired. Serves 6–8.

Cheese with Beer Soup

2 tablespoons margarine or butter
1 (14-ounce) package frozen mirepoix blend
1 (12-ounce) can beer
2 cups chicken broth
1 teaspoon seasoned salt
1 cup sour cream
1 cup cubed Monterey Jack cheese

Melt margarine in 2-quart saucepan over medium heat; cook vegetables till tender. Stir in beer; heat to boiling; reduce heat. Cover and simmer 10 minutes.

Stir in chicken broth and seasoned salt. Heat to boiling; reduce heat. Cover and simmer 30 minutes; remove from heat. Stir in sour cream and sprinkle with cheese. Serves 4 or 5.

A Mighty Fine Cheddar Cheese Soup

Ham and cheese in a bowl . . . can't beat it.

1 (12-ounce) package frozen seasoning blend (chopped onion, celery, pepper)
½ stick butter
½ cup chopped cooked ham
⅔ cup all-purpose flour
4 cups chicken broth
4 cups milk
½ teaspoon dry mustard
1 teaspoon Cajun seasoning
1 (2-cup) package shredded sharp Cheddar cheese

In large stockpot, cook frozen vegetables in butter till tender-crisp, but not brown; stir in ham. Add flour and cook, stirring constantly 3 minutes. Whisk in broth, and cook, stirring constantly, until soup thickens slightly. Add milk, mustard, seasoning, and cheese. Stir until soup is heated through and thick. Do not boil. Serves 8.

Mirepoix (mire pwa) is the French name for a combination of chopped onions, carrots, and celery. These three ingredients are commonly referred to as aromatics. Similar combinations may include leeks, parsnips, garlic, tomatoes, shallots, mushrooms, bell peppers, chiles, and ginger. It can be eaten raw, roasted, or sautéed with butter. Mirepoix is the flavor base for many dishes, particularly stocks, soups, stews, and sauces. The combination of onions, carrots, and celery is sold in frozen packages in supermarkets. This is similar to frozen seasoning blend, which is chopped onion, celery, and bell pepper.

Suavy Sweet Potato Soup

2 cups finely chopped onions
2 tablespoons butter
2 (28-ounce) cans cut sweet potatoes
2 cups milk, divided
¾ teaspoon curry powder
½ teaspoon salt
Dash of ground red pepper

Sauté onions in butter in large saucepan. Cook 6–8 minutes till soft.

Drain potatoes and blend in blender with onions, I cup milk, curry powder, salt, and red pepper until smooth. Return mixture to saucepan and stir in remaining I cup milk. Cook 5 minutes over medium-high heat till heated through. Serves 6–8.

Editor's Extra: Nice to sub chicken broth for milk, or use some of each.

Split Pea and Ham Soup

come home to a delicious pot of pea soup.

I pound ham hocks
I pound dry green split peas, rinsed
2 (14-ounce) packages frozen mirepoix blend
  (chopped onions, celery, carrots)
I–I ½ teaspoons curry powder
2 teaspoons Greek seasoning
6 cups water

Combine all ingredients in a 4-quart slow cooker. Cover and cook on LOW setting 10–12 hours or HIGH setting 5–6 hours. Remove ham hocks. When ham hocks are cool enough to handle, remove meat from bones; discard bones. Coarsely chop meat; stir into soup. Serves 6–8.

The Real Deal Basil and Tomato Soup

½ large onion, chopped
½ carrot, shredded
½ stick butter
4 large ripe tomatoes, peeled, seeded, chopped
⅓ cup sugar
½ cup lightly packed chopped fresh basil, divided
1 (14½-ounce) can chicken broth
Salt and pepper to taste
Parmesan (optional)

Sauté onion and carrot in butter in large saucepan over medium heat until onion is limp. Stir in tomatoes, sugar, and half the basil. Bring to a boil, stirring constantly. Reduce heat; simmer, covered, 15 minutes. Stir in chicken broth, remaining ¼ cup basil, and salt and pepper; cook until heated through. Garnish with Parmesan, if desired. Serves 6. *(See full-color photograph in first insert following page 64.)*

Basil is expensive to buy and seems to get "tired" so quickly. Buy a plant instead. It is very easy to grow. Basil goes so well with tomatoes, whether it is for a soup or salad. Marinate cut tomato slices and chopped basil in a little rice wine vinegar—the flavor is so wonderful you will want to grow it all the time.

Quick & Thick Tomato Soup

2 tablespoons margarine or butter
½ cup chopped onion
½ cup instant loaded baked potatoes (or any flavor)
2 (14½-ounce) cans diced tomatoes with roasted garlic
3 cups milk
2 teaspoons Greek seasoning

In large saucepan, melt margarine over medium heat. Add onion; cook 1–2 minutes until onion is tender-crisp. Add remaining ingredients; cook uncovered 8–10 minutes or until thoroughly heated and flavors are blended, stirring frequently. DO NOT BOIL. Serve immediately. Serves 4–6.

Editor's Extra: Want creamier? Whirl tomatoes in blender before adding.

25

President Franklin D. Roosevelt and his family were soup lovers. They kept a big steel soup kettle singing in the White House. They enjoyed cream soup for lunch and clear soup before dinner. The president was partial to fish soups, such as clam chowder and turtle soup.

Touch of Curry Tomato Soup

Easy and good!

½ cup chopped onion
2 teaspoons olive oil
2 (14½-ounce) cans stewed tomatoes with garlic and basil
1½ cups chicken broth
½ teaspoon curry powder
Salt and pepper to taste

Sauté onion in oil in saucepan. Stir in tomatoes, broth, curry powder, and salt and pepper. Bring to a boil; reduce heat; cover and simmer 10 minutes. Cool slightly.

Process mixture in food processor, half at a time, till smooth. Serve hot or chilled. Serves 4–6.

Tortellini Sorento Soup

3½ cups water
2 teaspoons chicken bouillon granules
1 (14½-ounce) can diced Italian tomatoes, undrained
1 (10-ounce) box frozen cut leaf spinach
1 (15½-ounce) can kidney beans, drained, rinsed
1 (9-ounce) package refrigerated cheese-filled tortellini
1 teaspoon seasoned salt

Combine water, bouillon, and tomatoes in a 3-quart saucepan. Bring to a boil over medium-high heat. Add spinach, beans, tortellini, and seasoning; return to a boil. Reduce heat and boil gently 5 minutes or until tortellini is tender and soup is heated thoroughly, stirring occasionally. Makes 4 (1¾-cup) servings.

Egg Drop Soup

Also called Egg Flower Soup, this looks very simple when you consider the ingredients, but the method is what makes the threads of egg silky rather than clumpy. The secret: Holler for a little help.

4 cups chicken broth or stock
Salt to taste
¼ teaspoon white pepper
2 eggs
2 small green onions, minced

Bring broth with salt and pepper to a boil. In a spouted 2-cup measure, beat eggs lightly so as not to make them foamy. Turn heat off once broth has boiled. Pour eggs in a light stream about 8 inches above the pot through the tines of a fork. You will probably need help at this point unless you somehow position the fork to rest over the pot on its own, as you need to stir in the same direction constantly while dropping the eggs into the broth. Add minced green onions to each cup before serving. Serves 4–5.

Creamy Chicken and Wild Rice Soup

1 (32-ounce) carton chicken stock
½ teaspoon poultry seasoning
2-3 boneless, skinless chicken breasts
1 bunch green onions, chopped
1 (8.5-ounce) package of pre-cooked seasoned
  white and wild rice
1 (14-ounce) can sliced carrots
1 (10-ounce) package frozen chopped spinach,
  thawed
½–1 cup half-and-half
Freshly ground black pepper to taste
Italian cheese blend, shredded (blend of
  Parmesan, Romano, and Asiago cheeses)

In a medium soup pot, combine chicken stock and poultry seasoning. Add chicken breasts and green onions. Bring to a boil, lower heat, and simmer, covered, for 30 minutes.

Remove chicken, shred, and return to the pot. Add rice, carrots, and spinach and bring back to a boil. Lower heat and continue to simmer 20 minutes. Right before serving, add enough half-and-half until soup is creamy. Stir in pepper, and sprinkle soup with cheese. Serves 8.

Chicken Soup with Rivels

A favorite in Pennsylvania Dutch country.

1 (3- to 3½-pound) chicken, cut up
6 cups water
1 medium onion, sliced
3 medium stalks celery, with leaves, finely
   chopped
1 medium carrot, chopped
1½ teaspoons salt
1 (15-ounce) can cream-style corn
2 hard-cooked eggs, finely chopped

Place chicken, water, onion, celery, carrot, and salt in Dutch oven. Heat to boiling; reduce heat. Cover and simmer about 1½ hours or until juice from chicken is no longer pink when pierced. Remove chicken; cool about 10 minutes, then remove chicken from bones; cut into bite-size pieces. Skim fat from broth; return chicken; stir in corn and eggs. Heat to boiling; reduce heat. Sprinkle with Rivels; stir into soup. Simmer uncovered 10 minutes.

RIVELS:
1 cup all-purpose flour
¼ teaspoon salt
1 egg

Mix all ingredients until mixture resembles coarse cornmeal.

Italian opera composer Giuseppe Verdi (1813-1901) wrote numerous operas including Rigoletto, La Traviata, and Aida. When he needed inspiration, he had a bowl of noodle soup.

The holy trinity of cajun and creole cuisine consists of chopped celery, bell peppers, and onions, and are a staple base for much of their cooking. Largely called "frozen seasoning blend," this trio of ingredients is chopped and combined, ready for throwing in the pot. So often used when creating sauces, soups, stews, and stir-fries, it is referred to as one ingredient . . . a trinity . . . a holy trinity, if the cooks say so, and they do!

Short-Cut Chicken Noodle Soup

A quick cure for whatever ails ya.

4 (14½-ounce) cans chicken broth
1 (14-ounce) can sliced carrots, drained
1 (12-ounce) package frozen seasoning blend (chopped onion, celery, pepper)
2 cups cut-up cooked chicken
1 cup uncooked medium noodles

Bring to a boil the broth, carrots, and seasoning blend in 4-quart Dutch oven. Cover and simmer about 15 minutes. Stir in chicken and noodles. Heat to boiling; reduce heat. Simmer uncovered 7–10 minutes or until noodles are tender. Sprinkle with parsley for garnish, if desired. Serves 6–8.

Tangy Chicken Soup

1 cup coarsely chopped red bell pepper
2 teaspoons chopped jalapeño
2 teaspoons red curry powder
2 tablespoons rice vinegar
2 tablespoons soy sauce
3 tablespoons packed brown sugar
1 (32-ounce) carton chicken broth
2 cups skinned, chopped rotisserie chicken

Combine all ingredients except chicken in a large saucepan. Boil, then reduce heat and simmer, uncovered, 5 minutes. Stir in chicken. Cook a few minutes, only until chicken is hot. Serves 4.

Cajun Bean and Chicken Soup

A simply throw-in-the-crockpot, come-home-to-great-smelling soup!

1 (16-ounce) can Great Northern beans, rinsed
1 (14-ounce) package frozen mirepoix blend
   (chopped onions, celery, carrots)
1 teaspoon Cajun seasoning
3 (14½-ounce) cans chicken broth
2½ cups chopped cooked chicken
1 (14½-ounce) can diced tomatoes with garlic,
   undrained

Combine beans, mirepoix blend, seasoning, and broth in a slow cooker. Cover and cook on LOW setting 8–10 hours, or HIGH setting 4–5 hours. Stir in chicken and tomatoes. Cover and cook another 30 minutes on HIGH. Serves 6–8.

Quick Chick Navy Bean Soup

2 boneless, skinless chicken breasts, cut up
1 teaspoon olive oil
1 (12-ounce) package frozen seasoning blend
   (chopped onion, celery, pepper)
2 teaspoons garlic and herb seasoning
2 cups chicken broth
1 (14½-ounce) can Creole cream-style navy beans

Cook chicken in oil in large stockpot 3–5 minutes, stirring a few times, on medium-high heat. Stir in remaining ingredients. Boil, then simmer 10 minutes. Serves 3–5.

Editor's Extra: If you can't find Creole cream-style beans, use regular, and mash or process lightly with some of the liquid.

Masa flour is often used to thicken a southwestern soup. If you don't happen to have any, just pulverize some Fritos—tastes great!

Soup à la Tortilla

2 (14½-ounce) cans diced Mexican tomatoes
1 (14-ounce) can sliced carrots
1 cup frozen chopped onion
1 cup water
1 (14½-ounce) can chicken broth
1 cup diced, cooked chicken
1 (4-ounce) can diced green chiles
⅛ teaspoon salt
2 (15-ounce) cans pinto beans
⅓ cup snipped fresh cilantro
Tortilla chips, broken

Combine tomatoes, carrots, onion, water, broth, chicken, green chiles, and salt. Bring to a boil; reduce heat. Cover and simmer 20 minutes. Add beans and cilantro. Heat thoroughly. To serve, ladle soup into bowls. Put a few tortilla chips in each soup bowl. Serve immediately. Serves 4–6.

In-A-Flash Tortilla Soup

6 (6-inch) corn tortillas, divided
2 teaspoons oil, divided
1 cup bite-size pieces cooked chicken breast
2 (14½-ounce) cans chicken broth
1 cup chunky salsa
1 (8-ounce) can whole-kernel corn, drained
1 cup shredded 4-blend cheese

Cut 2 tortillas into strips; toss in bowl with 1 teaspoon oil. Bake on pan in 400° oven 10 minutes till crisp; put aside. Finely chop remaining 4 tortillas. In large saucepan, heat remaining teaspoon oil; add chicken pieces; cook and stir 5–6 minutes. Add chopped tortillas and remaining ingredients, except cheese; boil, then simmer 15 minutes. Serve topped with cheese and toasted tortilla strips. Serves 4.

Creamy Chicken Taco Soup

4 boneless, skinless chicken breasts, cut
1 (32-ounce) carton chicken broth
1 cup frozen chopped onion
1½ teaspoons taco seasoning
1 (10-ounce) can Ro-Tel tomatoes
1 (14-ounce) can sliced carrots
1 (15-ounce) can whole-kernel corn
1 cup heavy whipping cream
1 (5-ounce) package tortilla strips
2 cups shredded Monterey Jack cheese

Simmer chicken, chicken broth, onion, and seasoning in a large stockpot for about 30 minutes. Add undrained tomatoes, carrots, and corn. Bring to a boil; lower heat, and slowly add whipping cream until soup is thick and creamy. Place strips and shredded cheese in bottom of soup bowl, then ladle soup over cheese. Serves 8.

When planning a meal, we often think of meat, potatoes or pasta, and a veggie, sometimes with a salad. All these same ingredients can go in one pot for a hearty nutritious meal. It's called soup!

Sassy Chicken Salsa Soup

1 (14½-ounce) can chicken broth
2 cups bite-size pieces skinned rotisserie chicken
1½ cups water
1–2 teaspoons chili powder
1 (11-ounce) can Mexicorn
1 cup chunky salsa
1 cup broken tortilla chips
½ cup shredded pepper-Jack cheese

Heat chicken broth, chicken, water, and chili powder in a 3-quart saucepan. Bring to a boil; reduce heat; simmer 8 minutes. Add corn; simmer another 5 minutes. Stir in salsa; heat through. Ladle soup into bowls. Top with chips and sprinkle with cheese. Serves 4–6.

spices can get dull and lose their flavor. Always keep them out of sunlight. And it's a good idea to write the date of purchase on the container. You can revitalize them by heating in a heavy skillet (no oil) very quickly.

Classic Taco Ranch Soup

FABULOUS for sure!

1 pound ground beef
1 (12-ounce) package frozen chopped onion
1 (1¼-ounce) package taco seasoning mix
1 (15-ounce) can cream-style corn
1 (14½-ounce) can diced tomatoes
1 (15½-ounce) can golden hominy
1 (15½-ounce) can kidney beans
1 (15½-ounce) can chili beans
1 (10-ounce) can Ro-Tel tomatoes
Tortilla chips
1½ cups grated Monterey Jack cheese

Brown beef and onion; drain. Stir in each remaining ingredient except chips and cheese, all cans undrained. Bring to a boil, then simmer 10 minutes or more. Serve garnished with chips and cheese, maybe add a dollop of sour cream.

Mighty Meaty Meatball Soup

Add toppings to your own taste.

1 (1-pound) package frozen cooked Italian meatballs
6 cups water
1 (12-ounce) can tomato juice
2 tablespoons instant beef bouillon granules
1 cup frozen mirepoix blend (chopped onions,
   celery, carrots)
1 cup dried tiny shell pasta
2 medium tomatoes, chopped
½ cup croutons

Bake meatballs in a baking pan at 375° for 15 minutes. In
a 5-quart Dutch oven, combine water and tomato juice.
Bring to a boil over medium-high heat. Add bouillon granules, meatballs, mirepoix, pasta, and tomatoes. Return to
a boil; reduce heat. Cook, uncovered, about 10 minutes or
until pasta is tender. Top individual servings with croutons. Serves 6–8.

Pepe Meatball Soup

1 (12-ounce) package frozen meatballs
1–2 tablespoons oil
2 (14½-ounce) cans beef broth
1 (8-ounce) can tomato sauce
⅓ cup chopped onion
1 clove garlic, minced
1 teaspoon Italian seasoning
¼ cup orzo or acini di pepe pasta

Brown meatballs in oil in skillet. Remove and drain. Bring
broth, tomato sauce, onion, garlic, and seasoning to a boil
in same skillet over medium-high heat. Add meatballs to
broth. Simmer, covered, 20–25 minutes. Add pasta; cook
10 minutes or until pasta is tender. Garnish servings with
parsley, if desired. Serves 4–6.

Freeze any left-over veggies in a "soup" container, ready to go right into your next soup pot.

Everything-But-The-Kitchen-Sink Soup

1 pound lean ground chuck, browned, drained
1 (12-ounce) package frozen seasoning blend (chopped onion, celery, pepper)
2 (16-ounce) packages frozen corn, beans, peas combo
2 (14½-ounce) cans diced tomatoes with garlic, basil, oregano, undrained
1 (14½-ounce) can beef broth
4–5 cups water
1 cup uncooked orzo pasta
1 cup Parmesan, Romano, Asiago cheese blend

Combine all ingredients except orzo and cheese in a stockpot; bring to a boil. Add orzo and reduce heat to a gentle boil for 15–20 minutes. Sprinkle each serving with grated cheese. Serves 6–8.

Tri-Color Pepper Soup

If you like stuffed peppers, you'll love this soup.

1 pound ground beef
1 onion, chopped
1 each: green, red, and yellow peppers, chopped
3 (10¾-ounce) cans tomato soup
3 soup cans water
1 (8-ounce) can tomato sauce
1 (10½-ounce) can beef broth
1 teaspoon brown sugar
⅓ cup uncooked white rice

Brown ground beef, onion, and peppers; drain well. Add remaining ingredients. Simmer, covered, on low until rice is cooked, 20–30 minutes. Serves 6–8.

Editor's Extra: Serve this over a small square of cornbread for a hearty meal.

Speedy Chili-Soup

1 pound ground beef
1 tablespoon dried minced onion
1 (15½-ounce) can red kidney beans, undrained
1 (10¾-ounce) can tomato soup
1 soup can water
2 teaspoons chili powder

Brown beef with onion in a saucepan over medium heat, stirring occasionally. Stir in remaining ingredients. Heat to boiling, stirring occasionally. Serves 6.

Red beans and rice was purportedly so loved by famous New orleans musician Louis Armstrong that he used to sign his letters, "Red beans and ricely yours."

Speedy Red Beans and Rice Soup

A new twist on a classic recipe.

1 pound smoked sausage, cut into ½-inch slices
1 (15½-ounce) can kidney beans, rinsed, drained
1 (14½-ounce) can stewed tomatoes with garlic
2 (14½-ounce) cans beef broth
½ cup chopped onion
1 teaspoon dried basil
1 teaspoon dried parsley flakes
2½ cups cooked rice

Combine all but rice in a large saucepan. Bring to a boil, then simmer, uncovered, 15–20 minutes. Serve in a soup bowl over a scoop of hot rice. Serves 6–8.

CIOPPINO (chuh-PEE-noh) is a rich Italian fish stew made with tomatoes and a variety of fish and shellfish, usually highly-spiced.

Ten-Minute Cioppino

1 tablespoon olive oil
1 (12-ounce) package frozen seasoning blend (chopped onion, celery, pepper)
2 teaspoons minced garlic
2 (14½-ounce) cans Italian-style stewed tomatoes, undrained
½ cup water
6 ounces fresh or frozen peeled, deveined shrimp
6 ounces fresh or frozen fish fillets, cut into 1-inch pieces
3 tablespoons chopped fresh basil

Heat oil in a large saucepan. Add frozen vegetables and garlic. Cook and stir 4–5 minutes. Stir in tomatoes and water. Bring to a boil. Stir in shrimp and fish; return to a boil; reduce heat. Simmer, covered, 2–3 minutes until fish flakes easily with a fork and shrimp turn opaque. Stir in basil. Serves 4–6.

Bayou Fish Soup

12 ounces fish fillets or peeled shrimp
1 (14½-ounce) can chicken broth
1 (8-ounce) carton sliced mushrooms
1 zucchini, halved, sliced
1 (12-ounce) bag frozen chopped onion
1–1½ teaspoons Cajun seasoning
2 (14½-ounce) cans stewed tomatoes with garlic, undrained
1 teaspoon lemon juice

Cut fish into 1-inch pieces; set aside. Combine broth, mushrooms, zucchini, onion, and Cajun seasoning in a large saucepan. Bring to a boil; reduce heat. Simmer, covered, 10 minutes or until vegetables are tender.

Stir in fish (or shrimp) and tomatoes. Bring to a boil; reduce heat. Simmer, covered, 4–5 minutes or until fish flakes easily with a fork or shrimp turn opaque. Remove saucepan from heat. Stir in lemon juice. Serves 6–8.

Pepper Snapper Soup

2 cups coarsely chopped red bell peppers
1 cup chopped onion
2 tablespoons olive oil
3 (14½-ounce) cans chicken broth, divided
¼ teaspoon each: salt, black pepper, cayenne
1 ¼ pounds red snapper, cut into 1-inch pieces
½ cup chopped parsley

Sauté peppers and onion in large saucepan in oil 4–5 minutes. Add 1 can broth; bring to a boil; reduce heat. Simmer, covered, about 20 minutes or until peppers are tender. Cool slightly.

Pour half the mixture into a blender and blend until nearly smooth. Pour back into saucepan and repeat with remaining mixture; return it to saucepan. Add remaining 2 cans broth, along with seasonings. Bring to a boil; reduce heat. Add fish; simmer, covered, about 5 minutes, or until fish flakes easily with a fork. Stir in parsley. Serves 4–6.

This is an old trick that bears repeating. If your soup tastes too salty, place a raw potato into the soup pot and simmer about 15 minutes. The potato absorbs the extra salt. Go ahead and eat the potato . . . .it will more than likely be quite tasty!

Your soup is only as good as your stock. Whatever liquid you use (broth, stock, wine, milk), make sure it is one you would want to drink. Homemade stock is best, of course, but quality canned broth, preferably low-sodium (so flavors of food will prevail) is available at your supermarket. Broths sold in boxes have an even better taste than canned.

Sea Scallops and Fried Corn Soup

This soup is so tasty and makes a lovely presentation.

1 (14½-ounce) can chicken broth
5 cups white corn, fresh or frozen, divided
1 cup half-and-half, divided
3 tablespoons butter
12 sea scallops, halved
¼ teaspoon Greek seasoning

Boil broth and add 4 cups corn; return to a boil; simmer 3 minutes. Purée in blender; add ¼ cup half-and-half, and blend till smooth. Return to saucepan and stir in remaining half-and-half.

Fry remaining 1 cup corn in butter over high heat in skillet (cover to keep from popping out of pan). Place browned corn on paper towel to drain. Sauté scallops in same skillet over high heat, searing all sides. Season.

Ladle simmering soup into wide shallow bowls, placing 4 scallop halves in center; sprinkle fried corn around scallops and grind black pepper over top for garnish. Serves 6.

Mai-Thai Good Shrimp Soup

Thai-style rice noodle mixes can be found in the Asian food section of grocery stores. The noodles come with seasoning packet and flavored oils.

I (28-ounce) carton chicken broth
I cup water
I small zucchini, cut into small chunks
I Thai-style rice noodle mix with lemongrass
I Thai-style rice noodle mix with ginger
$\frac{1}{4}$ teaspoon crushed red pepper
2 tablespoons chopped fresh basil
I pound medium frozen shrimp, thawed, peeled
$\frac{1}{2}$ cup sliced baby carrots
I cup snow peas
I (14-ounce) can unsweetened coconut milk (not cream of coconut)
I bunch green onions, chopped

In a medium soup pot, bring chicken broth and water to a low boil. Add chunks of zucchini; cover, and boil 5 minutes. Mix dry rice noodles with their seasoning packets and oils, then add to chicken stock. Add red pepper, basil, shrimp, carrots, and snow peas. Simmer 3 minutes, or until shrimp turns pink. Stir in coconut milk, and continue simmering until smooth. Toss in green onions right before serving. Sprinkle soup with toasted coconut, if desired. Serves 4. *(See full-color photograph in first insert following page 64.)*

Spicy Shrimp Soup

3 (14½-ounce) cans chicken broth
1 (12-ounce) package frozen peas and carrots
2–3 thinly sliced green onions
½ teaspoon Chinese five-spice seasoning
1 cup half-and-half
3 tablespoons all-purpose flour
8 ounces cooked, peeled, deveined shrimp,
   coarsely chopped
1 teaspoon Dijon-style mustard
Snipped fresh parsley

Combine broth, peas and carrots, green onions, and 5-spice seasoning in large saucepan. Bring to a boil. Reduce heat and simmer, covered, 5–7 minutes till vegetables are tender. Shake half-and-half and flour in a jar till smooth; stir into vegetable mixture; cook and stir over medium heat till bubbly. Stir in shrimp and mustard; heat through. Garnish servings with parsley. Serves 4–6.

Bisques

Minute Shrimp Bisque

2 (11-ounce) cans condensed tomato bisque
1 pint half-and-half
½ cup dry white wine, sherry, or water
1 (4-ounce) can tiny shrimp, drained

Heat tomato bisque and half-and-half to boiling over medium heat. Stir in wine and shrimp. Heat just until shrimp turn pink. Serves 8.

Smooth and Silky Shrimp Bisque

2 (10¾-ounce) cans cream of shrimp soup
1½ soup cans half-and-half
1 pound deveined frozen shrimp, thawed and peeled
1 tablespoon chopped fresh chives
½ teaspoon Chinese five-spice seasoning
2 tablespoons cooking sherry

In a medium soup pot, whisk soup and half-and-half until smooth. Simmer over low heat until almost boiling. Add shrimp, chives, and seasoning. Simmer about 5 minutes, but do not boil. Right before serving, add sherry. Serves 4.

Editor's Extra: Fat-free half-and-half works, too.

When adding wine to soups, you might want to bring it to a boil and let it cook for about 10 minutes to cook off the harshness of the alcohol.

Bisque is a rich, smooth, thick soup usually made with cream and shell-fish such as crab, shrimp, or lobster. It can also be made with puréed vegetables or poultry.

Lobsta Bisque

1 (1- to 1½-pound) fresh lobster, or 4 small
   lobster tails
2 quarts boiling water
1 (14-ounce) package frozen mirepoix blend
   (chopped onions, celery, carrots)
1 bay leaf
1 (48-ounce) carton chicken broth
2 tablespoons butter, melted
⅓ cup all-purpose flour
2 cups half-and-half

In large pot, cook "lobsta" in boiling water 3–8 minutes till bright pink. Drain; cool. Peel meat; cut into pieces; refrigerate. Break shell into pieces and boil in stockpot with remaining ingredients except butter, flour, and half-and-half. Reduce heat to medium; cook uncovered 20 minutes, stirring occasionally. Strain broth; discard vegetables and shell.

In small bowl, whisk butter, flour, and 3 tablespoons stock; whisk this into stockpot. Cook uncovered 10–15 minutes, stirring frequently.

Just before serving, stir in half-and-half and lobster meat. Cook uncovered over medium heat 10 minutes. Serves 6.

Crab Bisque the Easy Way
Elegant and easy!

1 (10¾-ounce) can cream of mushroom soup
1 (10¾-ounce) can cream of asparagus soup
3 cups milk
1 pint half-and-half
1 (6-ounce) package frozen crabmeat, thawed, or
   1 (7-ounce) can crabmeat, drained, flaked
3 tablespoons dry sherry

Combine soups, milk, and cream in a saucepan over medium heat until boiling, stirring frequently. Add crabmeat and sherry, and serve when heated through. Serves 6.

A Dilly of a Salmon Bisque

1 medium onion, chopped
1–2 tablespoons vegetable oil
1¼ cups water
½ cup uncooked long-grain rice
1 (14½-ounce) can chicken broth
6–8 ounces salmon fillets, cut into 1-inch pieces
2 cups fresh or frozen whole-kernel corn
1 (12-ounce) can evaporated milk
1 tablespoon Dijon-style mustard
½ teaspoon dried dill
Salt and pepper, or Greek seasoning to taste

Sauté onion in oil in large saucepan; cook and stir over medium heat until tender. Add water and bring to a boil; stir in rice. Reduce heat; simmer, covered, 15 minutes. Add broth; return to a boil. Add salmon and corn. Simmer, covered, 5 minutes or till salmon flakes easily. Stir in milk, mustard, dill, and seasonings; heat through. Garnish with fresh dill sprigs, if desired. Serves 4.

Big Taste Tomato Basil Bisque

2 (10¾-ounce) cans tomato bisque
1 (14½-ounce) can stewed tomatoes with basil
   and garlic, undrained
1 tablespoon chopped fresh basil leaves (optional)
½–1 cup fat-free half-and-half
Salt and pepper to taste

In a medium saucepot, combine tomato bisque and stewed tomatoes with juice (purée tomatoes first if you like a smoother-textured soup). Simmer over medium heat for 10 minutes; add fresh chopped basil leaves and simmer a few minutes more. Whisk in half-and-half until soup has desired creaminess. Season to taste. Serves 4.

chowder is a thick, chunky, satisfying soup. The term chowder comes from the French chaudière, meaning caldron. Fishermen cooked their food fresh from the sea in caldrons.

Veggie-Tortellini Chowder

1½ (16-ounce) packages frozen broccoli, cauliflower, and carrots
2 (14½-ounce) cans chicken broth
1 (9-ounce) package refrigerated cheese-filled
   tortellini
2 cups milk, divided
¼ cup all-purpose flour
1 cup shredded Gouda cheese
1 tablespoon chopped fresh basil
1 teaspoon Greek seasoning

Bring vegetables and broth to a boil in a large saucepan; add tortellini. Return to a boil; reduce heat. Simmer 4–6 minutes, just until vegetables are tender.

Shake 1 cup milk with flour in a covered jar; shake well. Stir into soup; add remaining milk. Cook and stir until slightly thickened. Cook and stir over medium heat 2–3 minutes more. Stir in cheese until melted. Stir in seasonings. Serves 6.

Quick Bean 'n Bacon Chowder

3 (15-ounce) cans navy beans
1 (3-ounce) package Real Bacon Bits
1 (14-ounce) can sliced carrots, drained
1 (12-ounce) package frozen seasoning blend
   (chopped onion, celery, pepper)
1 teaspoon Italian seasoning
1 (49-ounce) can chicken broth
1 cup milk

Combine all but milk in large pot; bring to a boil; stir. Add milk; cover and heat 10 minutes or until heated through. Serves 6–8.

Loaded Baked Potato Chowder

This is awesome! Bake a few extra potatoes when the occasion arises so you'll have some for this delicious soup.

1/3 cup butter
4 large baked potatoes, peeled, chopped
1 1/2 teaspoons garlic salt
5 green onions, chopped
1 cup sour cream
4 cups milk
1 cup grated Cheddar cheese
5 slices bacon, cooked, crumbled

Melt butter in large stockpot, then stir in remaining ingredients, except bacon. Heat through till cheese is melted, but do not boil. Garnish with bacon bits and additional grated cheese, if desired.

Editor's Extra: You can freeze baked potatoes by peeling, cubing, and putting in sealer bags. Thaw a bit before putting into soup.

Fast Potato and Ham Chowder

1 cup chicken broth
1/2 cup chopped frozen onion
1 (5-ounce) package instant potatoes
2 cups milk
1 tablespoon butter
1/4 teaspoon each: dried thyme and basil
Salt and pepper to taste
1 cup finely chopped cooked ham

Bring broth and onion to a boil; reduce heat and whisk in instant potatoes. Add milk, butter, thyme, basil, salt and pepper, and ham. Cook and stir until heated through. Serves 4.

47

Ham and Asparagus Chowder

2 medium red potatoes, peeled, cubed
$\frac{1}{2}$ cup water
1 (15-ounce) can asparagus, drained, cut
$1\frac{1}{2}$ cups cubed cooked ham
1 ($10\frac{3}{4}$-ounce) can cream of mushroom soup
1 cup milk
Freshly ground black pepper

Boil potatoes in water in a 2-quart saucepan. Reduce heat to medium; cover and cook 5–7 minutes till potatoes are tender-crisp. Add asparagus and ham; cover and cook 6 minutes. Stir in soup and milk; bring to a boil, then simmer. Sprinkle servings with pepper. Serves 4.

Broc & Chic Chowder

2 ($14\frac{1}{2}$-ounce) cans chicken broth
1 (1-pound) package frozen broccoli florets
2 cups light cream
1 (3-ounce) package cream cheese, cubed
2 cups chopped cooked chicken
1 teaspoon dried basil (or tablespoon snipped
  fresh)
Salt and black pepper to taste
$\frac{1}{2}$ cup shredded Swiss cheese

Boil broth and broccoli in a large saucepan; reduce heat. Simmer, covered, for 3 minutes.

Stir cream and cream cheese into soup. Cook and stir over medium-high heat until smooth. Stir in chicken, basil, salt and pepper; heat through, but do not boil. Sprinkle cheese over each serving. Serves 6–8.

Kicky Corn and Chicken Chowder

1 pound boneless, skinless chicken breasts, cut into ½-inch pieces
2½–3 cups thawed frozen whole-kernel corn
1 medium onion, coarsely chopped
1–2 tablespoons water
1 cup diced carrots
1–2 tablespoons finely chopped jalapeño (optional)
½ teaspoon dried oregano leaves
¼ teaspoon dried thyme leaves
2 (14½-ounce) cans chicken broth
1½–2 cups milk
½ teaspoon salt

Cook and stir chicken in saucepan sprayed with cooking spray (or a tad of oil) about 10 minutes or until no longer pink in center. Remove chicken. Add corn and onion; cook and stir until onion is soft. Process 1 cup corn mixture in food processor or blender, adding 1–2 tablespoons water; reserve.

Add carrots, jalapeño, if desired, oregano, and thyme to saucepan; cook and stir about 5 minutes or until corn begins to brown. Return chicken to saucepan. Stir in chicken broth, milk, reserved corn mixture, and salt; bring to a boil. Reduce heat to low and simmer, covered, 15–20 minutes. Serves 4–6.

Treat your knives well and they will stay sharper longer. Wash and dry them right after use—no leaving them in water, and no dishwashing.

49

Cream of Chicken Corn Chowder

4 boneless, skinless chicken breasts
3 (14½-ounce) cans chicken broth
2 teaspoons poultry seasoning
3 green onions, chopped
1 (15-ounce) can whole-kernel corn, undrained
1 (15-ounce) can cream-style corn
1 (14-ounce) can sliced carrots, drained
1½ cups frozen cubed hash brown potatoes,
  thawed
1 (3-ounce) package cream cheese, cubed
1½ cups half-and-half
Salt and pepper to taste

In a large stockpot, boil chicken breasts in chicken broth with poultry seasoning until tender and easy to shred. Remove chicken breasts, cut into small pieces, and return to pot at reduced heat. Add chopped green onions, all canned vegetables, and hash browns. Heat to boiling again and add cream cheese. Reduce heat and simmer until cream cheese cubes are melted. Stir in half-and-half, salt and pepper before serving. Serves 6–8.

Cheesy Corn & Crab Chowder

A wonderful combination of flavors . . .

1 ¼ cups frozen whole-kernel corn
1 cup chicken broth
½ cup sliced green onions
½ cup chopped green bell pepper
¾ teaspoon crushed dried basil
½ teaspoon white pepper
3 cups milk
3 tablespoons cornstarch
1–2 cups cooked fresh crabmeat
1 ½ cups shredded Swiss cheese

In a large saucepan, combine corn, broth, green onions, bell pepper, basil, and white pepper. Bring to a boil; reduce heat. Simmer, covered, 5 minutes. Stir together milk and cornstarch. Stir into hot mixture. Cook and stir until thickened and bubbly. Stir in crabmeat and cheese; heat and stir until cheese melts. Serves 8.

Editor's Extra: Heavy cream or half-and-half is sometimes substituted for some or all of the milk to make the chowder even thicker.

A bit of something fresh added just before serving can visually perk up the soup. Try fresh herbs, juice, sour cream, or yogurt.

Creamy Crab Chowder

creamy and divine.

**⅓ cup finely chopped onion
1 rib celery, finely chopped
1 stick butter
1 pound backfin crabmeat
1 egg yolk, hard-boiled, mashed
2 cups milk
1 cup half-and-half
1 teaspoon Greek seasoning
3 tablespoons dry sherry**

Sauté onion and celery in butter in saucepan over medium heat. Stir in crabmeat and chopped egg yolk; heat 2–3 minutes. Add milk, half-and-half, and seasoning. Heat, but do not boil. Simmer 20 minutes, stirring often. Just before serving, stir in sherry; heat and serve in warm bowls. Serves 4–6.

Hash Brown Oyster Chowder

**1½ cups finely chopped onions
⅛ teaspoon crushed dried thyme
3 tablespoons butter
2 cups frozen shredded hash brown potatoes
3 cups half-and-half
Salt and pepper to taste
1 pint raw oysters, undrained
2 tablespoons chopped fresh parsley**

Sauté onions and thyme in butter in a large saucepan over medium heat, stirring occasionally. Add hash browns and cook till tender, about 15 minutes. Add half-and-half, salt and pepper, and bring just to boiling, then add oysters and heat till oysters curl. Sprinkle with parsley and serve over oyster crackers, if desired.

Ahoy Mate Oyster Chowder

¾ cup chopped onion
2 tablespoons butter
3 tablespoons all-purpose flour
1 (14½-ounce) can chicken broth
2 red potatoes, peeled, cubed
2 cups half-and-half
1 (15-ounce) can cream-style corn
1 (7-ounce) can Niblets corn
2 (8-ounce) cans oysters, drained
2 tablespoons chopped fresh parsley

Sauté onion in melted butter in Dutch oven, stirring till soft. Add flour; cook 1 minute, stirring constantly. Stir in chicken broth and potatoes. Cover; cook 10–15 minutes or until potatoes are just tender, stirring occasionally. Stir in half-and-half, creamed corn, and Niblets. Cook uncovered 5–6 minutes or until mixture is hot, stirring occasionally. Stir in oysters and parsley; cook 5–6 minutes or just until oysters are thoroughly heated. Makes 6–8 servings.

Dog and Cheese Chowder

1 cup frozen whole-kernel corn
1 cup milk
2 (18½-ounce) cans cheese and potato soup
4 hot dogs, thinly sliced
1½ cups shredded Cheddar cheese, divided

Combine all but cheese in a 3-quart saucepan. Bring to a boil; simmer 7 minutes or until corn is tender, stirring frequently. Stir in 1 cup cheese. Top each serving with additional cheese. Serves 4–6.

President John F. Kennedy was fond of soups . . . New England fish chowder was a favorite. He has been described as a "soup, sandwich and fruit" man for lunch.

Easy Chicken and Crab Gumbo

A great make-ahead meal.

2 teaspoons minced garlic
3 tablespoons oil
3 tablespoons flour
4 cups chicken broth
2 (14-ounce) packages frozen gumbo vegetable mix
1 (14½-ounce) can diced tomatoes, undrained
⅓ cup quick-cooking rice
2 teaspoons Cajun seasoning
1 bay leaf
2 (6-ounce) packages grilled chicken strips, cut up
1 (6½-ounce) can crabmeat, drained (or fresh)

Sauté garlic in hot oil. Stir in flour till slightly brown. Add chicken broth, vegetable mix, tomatoes, rice, seasoning, and bay leaf. Bring to a boil; cover and simmer 10–15 minutes, or till okra is tender. Stir in chicken and crabmeat; heat thoroughly. Serves 6.

Short-Cut Shrimp Gumbo

1 (14½-ounce) can stewed tomatoes, undrained
1 (10¾-ounce) can chicken gumbo soup
1 (10-ounce) package frozen cut okra
1 cup water
1 teaspoon Cajun seasoning
1 (10-ounce) package frozen, peeled shrimp, thawed
¼ cup cooked bacon pieces
1 teaspoon filé powder (optional)
2 cups hot cooked rice

Combine all in a large pot. Bring to a boil; reduce heat. Simmer, covered, 10–20 minutes till okra is tender. Heat through. Serve over hot cooked rice. Serves 5–6.

"The word gumbo comes from the African word kingumbo, which means okra. And okra, a long, fuzzy green vegetable pod that came from Africa, is one of gumbo's characteristic ingredients. Besides being a tasty vegetable, it is a thickener. Then came filé (FEE lay), which can be traced back to the French market in New Orleans to be sold for medicinal purposes. The Creoles liked the delicate flavor and began using it in their soups and stews. They found that besides adding flavor, filé also thickened with the same slippery smoothness of okra, and could be substituted when okra wasn't in season.

(continued)

54

Slow-Cooker Gumbo

More like gumbo soup, this has good flavor and doesn't require as many steps as roux-based gumbo.

1 pound boneless, skinless chicken thighs
½ pound fully cooked smoked sausage, chopped
2 ribs celery, sliced
1 onion, chopped
1 (14½-ounce) can diced tomatoes, undrained
5 cups chicken broth
1 teaspoon Cajun seasoning
1 (10-ounce) box frozen cut okra, thawed, drained
½ teaspoon Tabasco
3 cups hot cooked rice

Mix all ingredients in a slow cooker except rice. Cook on LOW setting 7 hours. Spoon gumbo over rice in 6–8 soup bowls. Offer additional Tabasco.

(continued)
creole cooks began many of their dishes with a roux (ROO)—the slow browning of flour. They discovered roux gave additional thickening and flavoring to their gumbo."

From *The Little Gumbo Book* by Gwen McKee

Quick Gumbo

Don't hesitate to start with a mix; it's just a step saver to make things easier.

1 pound Cajun-flavored link sausage
2 tablespoons oil
2 tablespoons flour
7 cups water
1 box Zatarain's gumbo mix
1 cup sliced okra
1 (10-ounce) package frozen peeled, deveined
   shrimp, thawed
½–1 teaspoon Cajun seasoning (optional)

Slice or cube sausage and cook in Dutch oven or large skillet till lightly browned. In a cast-iron skillet over medium-high heat, add oil and flour. Brown, stirring constantly, till desired darkness. Add water, gumbo mix, and okra; stir till thoroughly mixed. Bring to a boil; turn down heat and cook 25–30 minutes; stir occasionally to keep from sticking. Stir in shrimp the last 10 minutes of cooking. May add Cajun seasoning, if desired.

Although gumbo mix has rice in it, you may want to serve the finished product over additional rice. Serves 6–8.

Mama's Old-Fashioned Stew

1–1½ cups cubed stew meat or roast, cooked
1 (48-ounce) carton beef broth
1 (14½-ounce) can diced tomatoes, undrained
2 medium potatoes, peeled, cut into 1-inch pieces
1 (12-ounce) bag frozen seasoning blend
  (chopped onion, celery, pepper)
2 cups shredded cabbage
1 (15½-ounce) can red kidney beans, rinsed,
  drained
1 (14-ounce) can cut green beans
1 cup chopped zucchini
1 teaspoon dried oregano
¼ teaspoon Tabasco

In Dutch oven, boil meat, broth, tomatoes, potatoes, and seasoning blend; reduce heat; simmer, uncovered, 15 minutes. Add cabbage, both beans, zucchini, oregano, and Tabasco. Simmer about 15 minutes more or until vegetables are tender. Salt and pepper to taste, if desired. Serves 6.

Editor's Extra: Frozen seasoning blend consists of diced onion, celery, and bell pepper, and is found in the frozen vegetable section of your grocery. If you can't find it, ask your grocer to carry it, as its convenience will make you want to keep it handy for many dishes that call for these chopped vegetables.

Stews are thicker, have less liquid, and are somewhat chunkier than soups. The same ingredients can be used, usually cut in larger chunks.

It is best to brown meat in a heavy pot (such as enamel cast-iron) before combining it with rest of ingredients for soup. This gives a nice color and leaves good drippings in bottom of pan that add to the flavor of your soup or stew.

Two-Step Stew

1 ¼ pounds beef stew meat, cut into 1-inch pieces
1 tablespoon oil
1 cup dry red wine or water
½ teaspoon Old Bay Seasoning
1 (14½-ounce) can beef broth
1 (14½-ounce) can stewed sliced tomatoes, undrained
½ cup uncooked rice
1 (16-ounce) package frozen California-style vegetables (broccoli, cauliflower, carrots)
1 medium onion, cut into wedges
1 (7-ounce) can sliced mushrooms, drained

STEP 1: Brown beef in oil in Dutch oven. Stir in wine, seasoning, broth, and tomatoes. Heat to boiling; reduce heat. Cover and simmer 40 minutes.

STEP 2: Stir in remaining ingredients. Bring to a boil; cover and simmer 20–25 minutes until vegetables are tender. Serves 4–5.

Easy Oven Stew

This beckons you with its wonderful smell, and rewards you with its flavor.

1½ pounds beef stew meat, cut into 1-inch pieces
⅓ cup flour
Salt and pepper to taste
1–2 tablespoons vegetable oil
1 (10¾-ounce) can cream of celery soup
1 (10¾-ounce) can beefy mushroom soup
1½ cups water
1 (16-ounce) package frozen stew vegetables
1 (4-ounce) jar whole mushrooms, drained
2 tablespoons dried onion flakes

Shake beef pieces in seasoned flour, and brown lightly in oil in Dutch oven. Stir in soups and water. Next, stir in stew vegetables, mushrooms, and onion flakes. Bake, covered, in 350° oven for 2–2½ hours or until beef and vegetables are tender. Serves 6.

Slow Oven Stew

Old-fashioned recipe . . . awesome taste!

2 pounds lean beef, cubed
1½ teaspoons Cajun seasoning, divided
2 onions, sliced
2 red potatoes, peeled, cut in big chunks
2 stalks celery, cut 1 inch
3 carrots, cut 1 inch
½ teaspoon sugar
¼ cup tapioca
1½ cups V-8 juice

Season meat with ½ the seasoning and put in Dutch oven. Add vegetables; sprinkle with remaining seasoning and sugar. Mix tapioca in V-8, then pour over all. Cover and bake at 250° for 5 hours, or 325° for 3½ hours. Don't peep! Serves 6.

59

Want your stew thicker? Dissolve 1 tablespoon corn-starch in ¼ cup water and stir into stew; heat and stir till it thickens.

Burgundy Bacon Beef Stew

2 pounds lean stew meat, cubed
I teaspoon salt
¼ teaspoon black pepper
2 tablespoons oil
2 tablespoons tapioca
2 (16-ounce) packages frozen stew vegetables
I (14½-ounce) can beef broth
⅔ cup Burgundy wine
2 teaspoons minced garlic
4 slices bacon, cooked crisp, crumbled

Season beef. Sear beef, half at a time, in oil in large skillet. Transfer to slow cooker. Sprinkle with tapioca. Stir in stew vegetables, broth, wine, and garlic. Cover and cook on LOW 10–12 hours or on HIGH 5–6 hours. Before serving, sprinkle crumbled bacon on each serving. Serves 6–8.

Editor's Extra: Can do in 325° oven, covered, for 2 hours.

Cola Beef Stew

I ½ pounds beef stew meat, cut into chunks
I (20-ounce) bag frozen stew vegetables
I (10¾-ounce) can tomato soup, undiluted
I tablespoon steak sauce
Salt and pepper to taste
I (8-ounce) can cola
Shredded Cheddar cheese

In large roasting pan, place beef and vegetables. Pour soup over all. Add steak sauce and salt and pepper to taste. Pour cola over top, but do not stir. Cover with tight fitting lid and bake at 250° for 5 hours. DO NOT OPEN OVEN. Serve in bowls; top with shredded cheese.

Porky Pig Black Bean Stew

1 pound boneless ham, cubed
¾ pound link pork sausage, cubed
¾ pound link Italian sausage, cubed
2 (15-ounce) cans black beans, rinsed, drained
2 cups water
2 tomatoes, chopped
1 medium onion, chopped
1 teaspoon red pepper flakes
6 cloves garlic, minced

Preheat oven to 350°. Combine all ingredients in large Dutch oven. Bring to a boil over high heat. Cover and place in oven. Bake 30 minutes; uncover and bake 30 minutes longer, stirring occasionally. Serve hot with cornbread. Refrigerate leftovers. Serves 8.

Cantastic Taco Bean Stew

A thick, satisfying stew.

1 pound lean ground beef
1 (15-ounce) can black beans
1 (15-ounce) can garbanzo beans
1 (15-ounce) can chili beans
1 (15½-ounce) can black-eyed peas
1 (14½-ounce) can Mexican-style stewed tomatoes
1 (11-ounce) can Mexicorn
1 (1¼-ounce) package taco seasoning mix
Sour cream, salsa, and broken tortilla chips

Cook beef in a 4-quart Dutch oven over medium-high heat until brown; drain off fat. Stir in undrained beans, peas, tomatoes, and corn; add taco seasoning. Bring to a boil; reduce heat. Simmer, covered, ½ hour or more, stirring occasionally. Top each serving with sour cream, salsa, and tortilla chips. Serves 8.

Southwest Chicken Stew

1 pound boneless skinless chicken breasts, cubed
2 cups chicken broth, divided
4 cloves garlic, finely chopped
1 tablespoon diced jalapeño
1 tablespoon all-purpose flour
1 red bell pepper, seeded, diced
1 carrot, peeled, sliced
1 cup frozen corn
Salt and pepper to taste
½ teaspoon ground cumin
2 tablespoons finely chopped fresh cilantro
Broken tortilla chips

In 4-quart heavy pot, cook chicken in ¾ cup broth till white. Remove chicken and set aside. Add garlic and jalapeño to broth in pot; cook over medium-high heat 2 minutes. Stir in flour and cook another 2 minutes, stirring constantly; gradually stir in remaining broth. Stir in chicken and remaining ingredients except tortilla chips. Heat to boiling; reduce heat. Cover; simmer 20–30 minutes, stirring occasionally. Serve sprinkled with broken tortilla chips. Serves 4.

Editor's Extra: Even easier to sub a jar of roasted red pepper, and a can of sliced carrots.

Good, Good Goulash

1 pound beef stew meat, cut into ¾-inch cubes
2 medium onions, cut into wedges
1 tablespoon oil
2½ cups beef broth
1 (14½-ounce) can diced Italian tomatoes
1 tablespoon paprika
¼ teaspoon thyme
¼ teaspoon pepper
3 medium potatoes, peeled, cubed
2 tablespoons snipped fresh parsley

Cook meat and onions in oil in Dutch oven until meat is brown. Stir in broth, tomatoes, paprika, thyme, and pepper. Bring to a boil; reduce heat. Cover and simmer 1 hour. Add potatoes. Cover and cook 25–35 minutes longer or till meat and potatoes are tender. Uncover the last 10 minutes to slightly thicken the mixture. Stir in parsley just before serving. Serves 4.

Vegetable peelers are so nice for fast peeling. Putting your veggies on a cutting board to do so makes it even easier.

Authentic Hungarian goulash (gulyas) is a beef dish cooked with onions, Hungarian paprika powder, tomatoes and some green pepper. It has a nice, evenly thick consistency like a sauce, somewhere in between a soup and a stew. Potatoes and noodles are also added to some recipes. Hungarian gulyas is usually eaten as a main dish.

Hungarian Goulash

This is the real thing!

1 pound boneless stew meat, cut into ½-inch cubes
⅔ cup chopped onion
2–3 tablespoons cooking oil
2 tablespoons flour
1 tablespoon Hungarian paprika (no substitute)
2 teaspoons minced garlic
3 (14½-ounce) cans chicken broth
1 (14½-ounce) can diced tomatoes, undrained
1 (14-ounce) can sliced carrots, drained
2 tablespoons tomato paste
1 bay leaf
½ teaspoon each: marjoram, caraway seeds, and black pepper
6 new potatoes, cubed

Brown beef and onion in oil in a 5-quart Dutch oven; cook over medium-high heat about 5 minutes. Add flour, paprika, and garlic. Cook 3 minutes. Stir in remaining ingredients except potatoes. Bring to a boil; reduce heat. Simmer, covered, 1 hour, stirring occasionally. Add potatoes; simmer, covered, 25–30 minutes, or till potatoes are tender. Remove bay leaf. Serves 6–8.

The Real Deal Basil and Tomato Soup (page 25)

Mai-Thai Good Shrimp Soup (page 41)

Hearty Home-Style Chili (page 65)

Chilled Peach Soup (page 71)

Hearty Home-Style Chili

2 pounds ground round
1 (14-ounce) package frozen mirepoix blend
   (chopped onions, celery, carrots)
1 (28-ounce) can diced tomatoes with garlic,
   oregano, and basil, undrained
1 (6-ounce) can tomato paste
½ tablespoon chili powder
2 teaspoons Cajun seasoning
2 (15½-ounce) cans red kidney beans, drained,
   rinsed

In large saucepan, brown beef; drain, then add frozen vegetables and tomatoes; cook till tender. Add remaining ingredients. Bring to a boil. Reduce heat; cover and simmer 1 hour. Serves 6 or 7. *(See full-color photograph in first insert following page 64.)*

Southwest Slow Cooker Chili

2 pounds chili ground beef
1 (12-ounce) package frozen chopped onion
¾ cup frozen chopped bell pepper
2 tablespoons minced garlic
4 cups water
1 (12-ounce) can tomato paste
1 (15½-ounce) can dark red kidney beans,
   drained
1 (16-ounce) can Great Northern beans, drained
1 (14½-ounce) can diced tomatoes, undrained
1 tablespoon yellow mustard
1½ tablespoons taco seasoning

Cook ground beef, onion, pepper, and garlic in a large skillet until brown. Drain. Put into a 6-quart slow cooker. Stir in water and tomato paste. Stir in beans, tomatoes, mustard, and seasoning. Cover and cook on LOW setting 8–10 hours, or HIGH setting 4–5 hours. Serves 8–10.

Hot Chili for Two

1 cup frozen chopped onion
2 teaspoons minced garlic
$\frac{1}{4}$ pound bulk hot Italian sausage
$\frac{1}{2}$ (14$\frac{1}{2}$-ounce) can stewed tomatoes, undrained
1 (5$\frac{1}{2}$-ounce) can spicy V-8 juice
1 teaspoon taco seasoning
1 (15$\frac{1}{2}$-ounce) can red kidney beans, undrained
Sour cream for topping

Cook onion, garlic, and sausage in a 2-quart saucepan over medium heat, stirring occasionally, till no longer pink. Stir in remaining ingredients except beans and sour cream. Heat to boiling; reduce heat. Cover and simmer 35–40 minutes, stirring occasionally. Uncover, add beans, and cook 20 more minutes, stirring occasionally. Top with sour cream, if desired. Serves 2.

Corny Chili

Doesn't get much easier or more delicious than this.

1 pound lean ground beef
1 (14$\frac{1}{2}$-ounce) can diced tomatoes, undrained
1 (15-ounce) can chili beans, undrained
1 (11-ounce) can Mexicorn, undrained

Brown beef in saucepan over medium-high heat until thoroughly cooked; stir frequently. Add remaining ingredients; mix well. Cook over medium heat 10–15 minutes, stirring occasionally. Serves 4–6.

Zesty Meatless Chili

2 (15½-ounce) cans red kidney beans, rinsed,
   drained
2 (15-ounce) cans garbanzo beans, rinsed, drained
2 (14½-ounce) cans beef broth
2 (11-ounce) cans Mexicorn, undrained
1 (10-ounce) can Ro-Tel tomatoes
1 cup chopped onion
1 tablespoon taco seasoning
½ cup sour cream
Corn chips

Combine all ingredients except sour cream and corn chips in a 4-quart saucepot. Bring to a boil; reduce heat; simmer, covered, 20 minutes. Top servings with sour cream, and crisp corn chip pieces. Serves 8.

Are cans shrinking? Years ago a "No. 2" can used to be a 16-ounce can. Today most cans weigh less. A rule of thumb is to just use the closest weight you can find.

Chunky Salsa Chili

Fun for guests to dish up their own bowls and garnish to taste.

1 tablespoon oil
¾ pound boneless pork, cubed
½ cup frozen chopped onion
2 (16-ounce) jars chunky salsa
2 (15-ounce) cans extra spicy chili beans
1 cup shredded lettuce
½ cup sour cream
1 (4-ounce) can chopped green chiles
½ cup shredded Cheddar cheese

Heat oil in Dutch oven over medium-high heat. Sauté pork and onion 5–10 minutes till pork is no longer pink, stirring frequently. Stir in salsa and beans. Reduce heat to medium; cover and cook 15 minutes, stirring occasionally. Ladle into bowls; top with shredded lettuce, sour cream, green chiles, and cheese. Serves 6.

White Chili in a Bread Bowl

1 cup chopped onion
1–2 (4-ounce) cans chopped green chiles, drained
2 teaspoons minced garlic
2 tablespoons oil
2 (16-ounce) cans Great Northern beans
4–5 cups chicken broth
1–2 teaspoons Cajun seasoning
1 (7-ounce) package grilled chicken strips,
 chopped
6–8 individual round loaves sourdough bread
Sour cream

Cook onion, chiles, and garlic in oil in Dutch oven till onion is tender. Stir in beans, broth, and seasoning. Bring to a boil. Simmer 30 minutes. Slightly mash beans to thicken. Add chicken; cover and simmer 10–15 minutes longer.

Hollow out sourdough loaves; spoon chili into bread bowls. Top with sour cream. Serves 6–8.

Blue Buffalo Chicken Chili

1 cup chopped onion
⅔ cup sliced celery
1 cup chopped red or yellow bell pepper
1 tablespoon oil
2 cups cut deli rotisserie chicken
1 cup chicken broth
1 tablespoon chili powder
5 or 6 drops Tabasco
2 (15-ounce) cans pinto beans, drained
1 (28-ounce) can crushed tomatoes, undrained
1 (14½-ounce) can diced tomatoes, undrained
½ cup crumbled blue cheese

Sauté onion, celery, and bell pepper in oil 5 minutes in saucepan over medium-high heat. Stir in remaining ingredients except blue cheese. Heat to boiling, then simmer 12 minutes or more, stirring occasionally. Top servings with blue cheese. Serves 6.

Editor's Extra: Sub 2⅔ cups frozen seasoning blend for onion, celery, and bell pepper to save time.

Three Bean Chicken Chili

Nice to serve with a chilled soup or jelled salad.

1 (15-ounce) can black beans, drained, rinsed
1 (15-ounce) can garbanzo beans, drained, rinsed
1 (15-ounce) can spicy chili beans, undrained
1 (14½-ounce) can diced Mexican-style tomatoes, undrained
1½ cups cubed cooked chicken
Sour cream and salsa

Combine all ingredients except sour cream and salsa in a 3-quart saucepan. Cook over medium heat for 10–12 minutes or until thoroughly heated, stirring occasionally. Top servings with sour cream and salsa. Serves 4.

Editor's Extra: You can make this serve more by serving over rice or ramen noodles.

Have your tomato plants been over-bearing? Wash and dry your extra tomatoes, and put them whole into plastic bags in freezer. When ready to use tomatoes in sauces, chilis, soups, or stews, dip frozen tomato in warm water for a few seconds—the peel slips right off. Chop or mash as desired.

chilled soups can be served before a meal, or as a palate refresher between courses.

Gotcha Gazpacho

colorful, cool, and refreshing, with a bit of a bite. Easy, too!

3 cups chopped tomatoes
½ cup chopped, seeded cucumber
1 tablespoon seeded, finely chopped fresh jalapeño
1 green onion, finely chopped
¼ cup finely snipped cilantro
1 clove garlic, minced
1 (16-ounce) can tomato juice
1 tablespoon olive oil
1 tablespoon lemon or lime juice
¼ teaspoon Tabasco
½ cup chopped cooked shrimp (optional)

Combine all but shrimp in a nonmetalic bowl. Cover and chill 1 hour or longer. Stir shrimp into chilled gazpacho; spoon gazpacho into chilled bowls. Top each with a dollop of sour cream, if desired.

Cool Carrot Soup

1 (16-ounce) package baby carrots
1 (14½-ounce) can chicken broth, divided
¼ teaspoon white pepper
Dash of ground ginger
½ cup sour cream

Cook carrots in boiling water for 20–25 minutes or till very soft; drain. Blend carrots and ½ cup chicken broth in a blender. Transfer carrots to a large mixing bowl. Stir in remaining chicken broth, pepper, and ginger. Cover and chill. Before serving, stir in sour cream. Top each serving with parsley, if desired. Serves 4–6.

Cool and Ready Red Pepper Soup

½ cup chopped onion
5 cloves garlic, chopped
1 tablespoon olive oil
1 medium potato, peeled, diced
½ red bell pepper, chopped (or jarred)
3 (14½-ounce) cans chicken broth
1 cup cottage cheese
½ teaspoon Old Bay Seasoning

Sauté onion and garlic in oil 3 minutes or till soft. Add potato, bell pepper, and chicken broth. Bring to a boil; reduce heat and simmer 10–15 minutes till potato is tender. Remove from heat; cool.

Process broth mixture in food processor or blender until smooth. Refrigerate until completely cool. Process cottage cheese until smooth. Set aside ¼ cup. Stir remaining ¾ cup cottage cheese and seasoning into chilled broth mixture until well blended. Top with reserved ¼ cup cottage cheese. Garnish with parsley, if desired. Serve chilled. Serves 6.

> "Good manners is the noise you don't make when eating soup."
> —Bennett Cerf

Chilled Peach Soup

Nice served with spicy foods or as a palate cleanser between courses.

1 (29-ounce) can sliced peaches
1 (8-ounce) carton sour cream
¼ teaspoon almond extract

Blend all; chill. Serves 4–6. *(See full-color photograph in first insert following page 64.)*

Editor's Extra: Drain peaches for a thick soup, then add juice to thin. Garnish with mint leaves or peach slices, as desired.

The culinary origins of vichyssoise, namely whether it is a genuinely French dish or an American innovation, is a subject of debate among culinary historians. credit for the dish usually goes to Louis Diat, the chef at the Ritz-Carlton in New York City in the 20th century. Others contend that French chef Jules Gouffé was first to create the recipe, publishing a version in Royal Cookery (1869). Diat may have borrowed the concept and added the innovation of serving it cold.

It is pronounced vee-she-SWAHZ in France, but Americans shortened it to vee-she-SWAH.

Chilly Cranberry Soup

4 cups fresh cranberries
3 cups water
1½ cups sugar
½ teaspoon pumpkin pie spice
1 tablespoon thin orange peel
2 tablespoons lemon juice

Combine cranberries, water, sugar, and seasoning in 3-quart saucepan. Bring to a boil; reduce heat. Simmer, uncovered, about 5 minutes or till half the cranberries are popped. Stir in orange peel and lemon juice. Cool. Chill before serving. Ladle soup into bowls. Garnish with mint leaves, if desired. Serves 6–8.

Editor's Extra: Good to heat some and serve as a gravy over turkey, chicken, duck, or venison.

Vichyssoise

1 tablespoon butter
½ cup sliced leeks or chopped onion
2 medium potatoes, peeled, sliced
1 (14½-ounce) can chicken broth
¼ teaspoon salt
⅛ teaspoon white pepper
¾ cup milk
½ cup whipping cream

Heat butter in saucepan; cook leeks or onion till tender. Stir in potatoes, chicken broth, salt, and pepper. Bring to a boil; reduce heat. Cover and simmer 20–25 minutes or till potatoes are tender. Cool slightly. Blend mixture in food processor till smooth. Pour into a bowl; stir in milk and cream. Cover and chill. To serve, top with snipped chives, if desired. Serves 4–6.

Salads

Green Salads

Picnic Salads

Fruit and Gelatin Salads

Pasta and Rice Salads

Meat and Seafood Salads

Salad Dressings

Robert Cobb, the owner of the Brown Derby restaurant in Hollywood, created the Cobb salad in 1936. Originally it contained chopped lettuce, avocado, celery, tomatoes, and strips of bacon. Later he embellished it with chicken, chives, hard-boiled egg, and watercress, and put Roquefort cheese in the dressing. Cobb salad and Caesar salad were the first "main course" salads in the United States, both being a huge jump from the meager greens and tomatoes with vinegar and oil dressing.

Classic Cobb Salad

1 head iceberg lettuce, shredded
3 cups chopped, cooked chicken
3 hard-boiled eggs, chopped
2 tomatoes, seeded, chopped
¾ cup blue cheese, crumbled
8 slices bacon, cooked, crumbled
1 avocado, peeled, pitted, cut in small pieces
3 green onions, chopped
1 (8-ounce) bottle vinaigrette or ranch dressing

Make beds of shredded lettuce on 8 salad plates. On each plate, arrange chicken, eggs, tomatoes, blue cheese, bacon, avocado, and green onions in rows on top of the lettuce. Drizzle with dressing.

Editor's Extra: See page 133 for Brown Derby's Cobb Salad Dressing.

Photo by Chalmers Butterfield

The Brown Derby restaurant

BLT Salad

1 medium tomato, cut into wedges
6 cups torn lettuce
⅓ cup Thousand Island dressing
2 slices cooked bacon, crumbled
1 hard-cooked egg, chopped

Toss all ingredients in bowl. Serves 4.

Editor's Extra: You can sub 2 tablespoons Real Bacon Bits to make it even quicker.

To remove core from iceberg lettuce, hold the head so that the bottom, or core end, faces cutting board, then bring lettuce down hard against counter to loosen core. Pull out core and discard. Do not cut lettuce, but rather pull and tear apart.

Fabulous Fontina Salad

SALAD:
4–5 cups mixed greens
1–2 cups cherry tomatoes, cut in half
6 ounces fontina cheese, cubed
1 small zucchini, sliced thinly
½ cup croutons
⅓ cup salad olives
½ cup walnut halves, toasted

Layer ingredients on a large platter.

FONTINA DRESSING:
¼ cup oil
2 tablespoons raspberry vinegar
1 tablespoon Dijon mustard
1 tablespoon sugar
¼ teaspoon salt
⅛ teaspoon black pepper

Mix or shake all ingredients in a jar. Pour over Salad and toss gently just before serving. Serves 8.

The Best Romaine Salad

I head romaine lettuce, torn
I (11-ounce) can Mandarin oranges, drained
I (8-ounce) can sliced water chestnuts, drained
I cup chopped celery
2 green onions, thinly sliced
$\frac{1}{3}$ cup vegetable oil
$\frac{1}{4}$ cup raspberry vinegar
$\frac{1}{4}$ cup sugar
$\frac{3}{4}$ teaspoon salt
$\frac{3}{4}$ teaspoon pepper
$\frac{1}{2}$ teaspoon Tabasco
$\frac{1}{2}$ cup broken pecans, toasted

Combine lettuce, oranges, water chestnuts, celery, and green onions in large salad bowl. Next, combine oil, vinegar, sugar, salt, pepper, and Tabasco in a jar; shake well. Just before serving, sprinkle pecans and dressing over salad; toss to coat. Serves 8–10.

Simply Italian Salad

I package romaine lettuce, torn
I (6-ounce) jar marinated artichoke hearts, drained
I (6-ounce) jar button mushrooms, drained
2 plum tomatoes, cut into wedges
$\frac{1}{2}$ cucumber, seeded, sliced
$\frac{1}{3}$ cup vinegar and oil or Italian salad dressing

Combine all ingredients except vinegar and oil and toss to mix. Drizzle with vinegar and oil; toss again to coat. Serves 4–6.

Blue Cheese Salad

I soft pear, peeled, halved, cored
6 cups mixed baby greens
½ cup crumbled blue cheese
½ cup walnut halves, lightly toasted
3 tablespoons olive oil
I tablespoon balsamic vinegar
Salt and pepper to taste

Slice pear halves lengthwise. Toss greens with blue cheese, walnuts, oil, and vinegar. Season. Arrange on 4 salad plates. Top with pear slices. Serves 4.

Touch of Tuscany Salad

2 cups torn red leaf lettuce
2 cups torn fresh baby spinach
I medium yellow or green bell pepper, cut into strips
½ cup chopped green olives
I small red onion, sliced, separated into rings

Toss together lettuce, spinach, peppers, olives, and onion.

TUSCANY DRESSING:
2 tablespoons red wine vinegar
2 tablespoons olive oil
I tablespoon water
1½ teaspoons garlic salt

Combine all in a jar. Cover and shake well. Sprinkle Tuscany Dressing over salad; toss lightly to coat. May sprinkle with freshly ground black pepper and Parmesan, if desired. Serves 4–6.

Blue cheeses are considered an acquired taste. They have penicillium cultures added so that the final product is spotted or veined with blue, blue-gray, or blue-green mold, and has a distinct smell. They are typically aged in a temperature-controlled environment such as a cave.

Pretty-As-A-Picture Spinach Salad

colorful and flavorful.

STRAWBERRY DRESSING:

3 tablespoons apple juice

2 tablespoons strawberry jam

2 tablespoons balsamic vinegar

Blend all ingredients and set aside.

SALAD:

1 boneless, skinless chicken breast

1 (10-ounce) package fresh spinach

12 fresh strawberries, stems removed, cut in thirds

3 tablespoons crumbled feta cheese

¼ cup chopped pecans

Cook chicken breast over medium-high heat in skillet 15–20 minutes, turning once, until juice of chicken is clear when cut in thickest part. Remove chicken; slice thinly in strips. Pour dressing in same skillet but do not heat; stir to loosen any pan drippings. Arrange spinach on 4 or 5 plates. Top with chicken, strawberries, and feta. Drizzle with dressing; sprinkle with pecans.

Strawberry Brie Salad

1 large bunch romaine lettuce, torn
1 (3-ounce) wedge Brie cheese, chopped
1 pint fresh strawberries, sliced
⅔ cup sliced almonds
2 tablespoons butter
1 tablespoon sugar

Place lettuce in salad bowl. Place Brie around edge of lettuce; place strawberries in center. Sauté almond slices in butter and sugar till just lightly browned; sprinkle over salad.

POPPYSEED DRESSING:
1½ tablespoons grated onion
1 cup oil
¾ cup sugar
1 teaspoon dry mustard
¼ teaspoon salt
½ cup vinegar
3 teaspoons poppyseed

Combine ingredients; mix well. Toss with salad.

Cranberry Feta Green Salad

1 large bag spring mix or baby greens
1 cup toasted pecans
½ cup dried cranberries
½ cup crumbled feta cheese
½ cup raspberry vinaigrette

Empty greens into salad bowl. Add pecans, cranberries, and feta cheese. Toss well. Drizzle with vinaigrette. Toss and serve. Serves 8.

one cup of strawberries contains approximately 45 calories and is an excellent source of vitamin c and flavonoids, which are known for their antioxidant properties.

Don't be afraid to mix bought dressings. Test small amounts to see how you like it. Interesting to drizzle one kind on greens, another on veggies and fruits that top it.

An Un-beet-able Combo Salad

6 cups torn fresh leaf lettuce and baby spinach combo
1 (8-ounce) can beets, chilled, drained, julienned
1 (16-ounce) can Mandarin oranges, drained
$\frac{1}{2}$ medium cucumber, thinly sliced
$\frac{1}{2}$ cup Italian salad dressing
3 tablespoons poppyseed dressing

Place greens on 6 salad plates; top with beets, oranges, and cucumber slices. Drizzle with Italian dressing, then thinly with poppyseed dressing. Serves 6.

Celestial Salad

Golf friend, Vera Everett, swears by this delicious salad.

1 head lettuce, torn into bite-size pieces
1 (11-ounce) can Mandarin oranges
1 cup halved green grapes
$\frac{1}{2}$ cup chopped green onions
$\frac{1}{2}$ cup sliced almonds, toasted

Combine all ingredients in large glass salad bowl. Just before serving, toss with Celestial Dressing. Serves 6–8.

CELESTIAL DRESSING:
$\frac{2}{3}$ cup vegetable oil
$\frac{1}{3}$ cup orange juice
$\frac{1}{4}$ cup sugar
3 tablespoons vinegar
1 teaspoon celery seeds
2 tablespoons chopped parsley
Salt to taste
Lemon pepper to taste
Dash of dry mustard

Combine all ingredients well. Gently toss with salad.

Spinach and Roasted Red Bell Pepper Salad

4 cups torn fresh spinach
1 (7¼-ounce) jar roasted red bell peppers, drained, cut into strips
1 medium zucchini, cut into thin strips
1 cup diced provolone cheese
½ cup seasoned croutons
½ cup raspberry vinaigrette

Arrange spinach in a large salad bowl or serving platter. Top with peppers, zucchini, cheese, and croutons. Toss with vinaigrette before serving. Serves 4.

Mandarin Spinach Salad

APRICOT VINAIGRETTE:

¼ cup apricot jelly
3 tablespoons red wine vinegar
1 teaspoon yellow mustard

Cook ingredients in small saucepan, stirring until jelly melts. Refrigerate to cool. Or chill in freezer 10 minutes.

SALAD:

6 cups fresh spinach leaves, stems removed
1 cup halved fresh strawberries
1 (11-ounce) can Mandarin oranges, drained
1 green onion, thinly sliced

In large bowl, combine all ingredients. Drizzle Apricot Vinaigrette over spinach mixture; toss to coat. Serves 4–6.

Although the United States ranks first in the world in strawberry production, about half of all strawberries are grown in Europe, where a woodland variety was harvested for market as early as 1600. Commercial production began in California in the 1850's, but didn't expand until 1900 or so when refrigerated railroad cars enabled growers to transport berries over long distances.

81

Caesar salad is a classic recipe that was created in the 1920's by Cesar Cardini in Tijuana, Mexico. It did not contain anchovies, but worcestershire gave it the slight anchovy flavor ... the anchovies were added later. The raw egg called for in the original recipe began to pose health problems, so now a coddled egg or yogurt (to give it creaminess) is most often used. Purists claim the acidic lime or lemon juice kills the bacteria, and insist the raw egg should be left in.

Sassy Caesar Salad

DRESSING:
1 coddled egg (boiled 1 ½ minutes)
¼ cup olive oil
¼ cup oil
3 teaspoons lemon juice
1 tablespoon Worcestershire
2 garlic cloves, pressed
1 teaspoon Dijon mustard
Salt and pepper to taste

Combine all ingredients; beat well.

2 heads romaine lettuce, washed, dried, torn
½ cup grated Parmesan cheese
3 anchovy fillets, cut up
½ cup croutons

Pour Dressing over lettuce in large salad bowl. Sprinkle with Parmesan cheese and toss. Add anchovies and croutons.

Wilted Greens 'n Bacon Salad

Fresh tender greens are the secret to this special salad.

4 cups torn tender fresh mustard and/or baby
**   spinach greens**
2 hard-boiled eggs, chopped
2 or 3 green onions, chopped
2 or 3 slices bacon, cooked, crumbled (reserve
**   drippings)**
Salt and pepper to taste

In large salad bowl, mix greens with eggs, onions, and bacon. When ready to serve, heat bacon drippings and pour over salad; toss till well coated. Salt and pepper to taste. Serve immediately.

Traditional Broccoli Salad

1 pound fresh raw broccoli florets
½ cup raisins
1 cup halved seedless red grapes
3 green onions, thinly sliced
½ cup grated Swiss or Cheddar cheese (optional)

Wash broccoli and cut tops into bite-size florets. Drain well. Soak raisins in a cup of hot water for 5 minutes; drain. Combine broccoli, raisins, grapes, and green onions in a large bowl. Add cheese, if desired.

BROCCOLI DRESSING:
¾ cup mayonnaise
2–3 tablespoons sugar
2–3 tablespoons tarragon, white wine, or apple cider vinegar
6–8 slices bacon, cooked crisp, crumbled
Slivered almonds

Mix mayonnaise, sugar and vinegar together. Stir until sugar is dissolved. Add to broccoli mixture. Cover and refrigerate at least 2 hours. At serving time, add bacon and almonds and toss again. Serves 6.

Jolly Good English Pea Salad

1 (15-ounce) can English peas, drained
2 hard-boiled eggs, chopped
½ cup finely chopped celery
1 teaspoon minced onion
1 teaspoon sweet pickle relish
3 tablespoons mayonnaise
1 teaspoon seasoned salt

Mix all well. Chill before serving. Serves 2–4.

Salad Nicoise (knee-SWAHZ) consists of potatoes, olives, and green beans, with a vinaigrette. Sometimes lettuce is the base and sometimes tomatoes.

Cranberry Carrot Salad

2 medium carrots, grated
¼ cup chopped walnuts or pecans
¼ cup dried sweetened cranberries
2–3 tablespoons mayonnaise
½ teaspoon sugar
Dash of salt and pepper

Stir carrots, nuts, and cranberries in a bowl. Combine mayonnaise, sugar, salt, and pepper in small bowl; mix with carrot mixture. Serves 4.

Mama's German Potato Salad

Mama started making this back in the 50's, and it's still the best around.
—Melinda Burnham

6 large red potatoes, boiled, drained, sliced
6 strips bacon, diced
¼ cup chopped onion
¼ cup chopped celery
1 tablespoon dill pickle relish
½ (12-ounce) bag shredded cabbage
¼ cup water
½ cup vinegar
½ tablespoon sugar
½ teaspoon salt
⅛ teaspoon paprika
¼ teaspoon dry mustard
Chopped parsley or chives for garnish

Place potatoes in a large bowl. Brown bacon pieces in a skillet until crisp; drain on paper towels.

Cook onion, celery, dill pickle, and cabbage in bacon drippings until limp; add bacon. In a separate saucepan, heat water, vinegar, sugar, salt, paprika, and mustard; pour these ingredients over bacon mixture. Immediately pour all over potatoes and toss to coat. Add parsley or chives.

Editor's Extra: Make this easier by using ½ cup frozen seasoning mix for the chopped celery and onion.

Best on the Deck Potato Salad

This goes so well with anything cooked on the grill, especially steaks and hamburgers.

DECK DRESSING:

¾ **cup mayonnaise**

½ **cup sour cream**

2 tablespoons steak sauce

2 tablespoons spicy brown mustard

1 tablespoon sherry or other wine-flavored vinegar

Mix all in a large bowl.

SALAD:

4 pounds small red potatoes, boiled, quartered

2 celery ribs, diced

½ **cup minced red onion**

¼ **cup chopped fresh parsley**

Salt and pepper to taste

6 slices lean snipped bacon, cooked crisp

A sprinkling of cayenne pepper

Fold potatoes while still warm into Deck Dressing. Let stand until cool. Add celery, onion, parsley, salt and pepper. Garnish with crumbled bacon and cayenne pepper. Serves 8–10.

When you need it cooked and crumbled, cut bacon before cooking—keeps you from burning your fingers trying to crumble while bacon is hot. Use scissors to easily cut bacon—no need to separate the slices.

85

My sister-in-law, Lois, not only made the best potato salad, but it always looked so pretty and inviting. She chilled the boiled potatoes before peeling and cutting. Then she squeezed a little fresh lemon juice over the potatoes. After that she added the celery and eggs and pickles and seasonings, and mixed it with a fork before adding the mayonnaise. I do it that way to this day.

—Gwen

Ranch, Bacon, 'n Tato Salad

10–12 small red potatoes, quartered
1 teaspoon salt
15 grape tomatoes, halved
1 rib celery, chopped
2 green onions, chopped
4 strips bacon, cooked, crumbled
½ cup ranch dressing

Bring potatoes to a boil in salted water to cover; reduce heat, cover, and simmer 10–15 minutes or till tender. Drain; rinse with cold water to cool. Drain well. When cool, place potatoes in covered bowl; add tomatoes, celery, onions, and bacon. Stir in ranch dressing. Serve warm or cool. Serves 8–10.

All American Potato Salad

¾ cup mayonnaise or Miracle Whip
2 teaspoons mustard
5–6 red or gold potatoes, boiled, peeled, cubed
3 boiled eggs, chopped
2-3 stalks celery, chopped
¼ cup diced onion
½ cup sweet pickle relish
Salt and pepper to taste

Mix mayonnaise and mustard in a large bowl. Add cooled potatoes, eggs, celery, onion, and relish; mix lightly. Season to taste with salt and pepper. Refrigerate. Garnish with celery leaves, if desired. Serves 6.

Editor's Extra: Exact amounts are hard to calculate since potato quantity varies. Taste and add.

Mose's Just Right Coleslaw

Best made several hours before serving so that flavors mingle.

½ head cabbage, shredded
¼ cup finely shredded carrot
2 tablespoons minced onion
¼ cup mayonnaise
1 tablespoon dill pickle juice or vinegar
3 teaspoons sugar
½ teaspoon salt

Combine vegetables in large mixing bowl. Combine remaining ingredients and pour over; mix well. Refrigerate. Serves 4.

Fruit and Nut Slaw

4 cups shredded cabbage
1 medium red apple, diced
⅓ cup chopped toasted pecans or almonds
2 tablespoons raisins
½ cup mayonnaise
2 tablespoons milk
2 tablespoons sugar
1 tablespoon lemon juice
Salt to taste

Combine cabbage, apple, nuts, and raisins; set aside. Combine remaining ingredients in a jar with a tight-fitting lid; shake well. Pour over salad and toss gently. Serves 6–8.

coleslaw was probably consumed, in its earliest form, in the times of the ancient Romans. The term "cole slaw" dates back to the 18th century, coming from the Dutch term "kool-sla," short for "kool-salade," which means "cabbage salad." The Brits called it "cold slaw" until the 1860's when "cole" was revived, which it is widely called today. Southerners, however, simply call it "slaw."

Pineapple Coleslaw

4 cups shredded cabbage
1 (15-ounce) can crushed pineapple, partially drained
¼ cup shredded carrot
1 green onion, diced
¼ cup chopped green bell pepper
⅔ cup mayonnaise
¼ cup sour cream
Salt and pepper to taste

Stir all together well. Refrigerate, covered, if not serving right away. Serves 8–10.

Editor's Extra: Add a ⅓ cup raisins or craisins and a ⅓ cup salted cashews or peanuts for variation.

Cabbage Pepper Slaw

A make-ahead, eat-when-you're-ready salad!

CABBAGE DRESSING:
¼ cup oil
2 tablespoons red wine vinegar
1 clove garlic, minced
1 tablespoon each: fresh oregano, basil, parsley
½ teaspoon dried oregano
1 teaspoon freshly ground black pepper
½ teaspoon salt

Whisk ingredients together. Pour over Cabbage Salad; toss thoroughly. Cover and refrigerate. Best after at least 4 hours; good for 4 days.

CABBAGE SALAD:
½ small head cabbage, finely shredded
1 bell pepper, julienned
¼ cup chopped purple onion

Toss vegetables in bowl. Serves 6–8.

Honey Apple Coleslaw

1 (16-ounce) bag coleslaw mix
3 green onions, chopped
1 Granny Smith apple, peeled, cored, cut into
   thin sticks
1 cup honey-mustard dressing

Toss ingredients in large bowl. Serve immediately, or cover and refrigerate up to 24 hours before serving. Serves 10–12.

Easy Oriental Slaw

ORIENTAL DRESSING:
½ cup oil
½ cup sugar
¼ cup rice wine vinegar
2 teaspoons salt
½ teaspoon pepper
½ teaspoon ground ginger

Combine all ingredients in a jar with tight-fitting lid. Shake to mix.

SLAW:
½ cup chopped almonds
1 (16-ounce) package coleslaw mix
1 cup grated carrots
⅓ cup chopped green onions
2 (3-ounce) packages ramen noodles, broken
2 tablespoons sunflower seed kernels

Toast almonds on baking sheet at 350° for 5 minutes or until lightly browned. In salad bowl, layer coleslaw mix and carrots. Pour dressing over top. Layer with onions, ramen noodles, almonds, and sunflower seeds. Chill, covered, 2 hours. Toss just before serving. Serves 10.

The regular grocery-store variety of curry powder is usually yellow from the turmeric. An ethnic or foreign food section of your supermarket is where you'll find the better red and green curries.

Kicked-Up-A-Notch Egg Salad

2 hard-boiled eggs, diced
2–3 tablespoons mayonnaise
Salt and pepper to taste
2 tablespoons finely chopped chives
½–1 teaspoon red curry powder
Lettuce leaves or toasted bread
2 tablespoons chopped pecans or almonds

Combine eggs, mayonnaise, salt and pepper, chives, and curry powder. Serve on lettuce leaves and top with chopped nuts for salad (or on toast for sandwich). If desired, sprinkle with a little red curry powder as garnish. Serves 2.

Muffuletta Salad

The muffuletta sandwich originated in New Orleans in the early 1700's. Here's a similar taste in a salad.

1 (12-ounce) jar marinated artichoke hearts, drained, chopped
5–6 slices salami, cut
¾ cup Italian olive salad
1 large tomato, cut into small wedges
1 (10-ounce) package Italian-blend mixed salad greens
⅓ cup zesty Italian dressing
4 ounces mozzarella cheese, diced
¾ cup garlic croutons

Toss all together lightly in large salad bowl. Serves 4–6.
(See full-color photograph in second insert following page 128.)

90

Basil Trayed Tomatoes

1 ½ tablespoons balsamic vinegar
¼ cup olive oil
1 tablespoon chopped fresh basil
1 teaspoon Dijon mustard
½ teaspoon salt
⅛ teaspoon pepper
4 medium tomatoes, sliced
12 ounces fresh mozzarella, sliced

Whisk vinegar, oil, basil, mustard, salt, and pepper together. Alternate tomatoes and cheese slices on a small tray or platter. Pour dressing mixture over top. Garnish with additional basil leaves and cracked black pepper, if desired. Serves 4–6.

Italian Summer Salad

Serve this with Italian bread slices for dipping.

4 Roma tomatoes
½ medium onion, sliced
½ cup pitted black olives
2 sprigs fresh basil, or ¼ teaspoon dried basil
Salt and pepper to taste
2 tablespoons olive oil
1 tablespoon balsamic vinegar
3 tablespoons ice water

Cut tomatoes into quarters. Place in glass salad bowl. Add sliced onion, olives, basil, salt and pepper, oil, and vinegar. Add water and toss again. Serves 4.

chill your serving plates to keep your salad crisp longer.

Succotash Salad

Pretty in Bibb lettuce cups on a salad plate, or in colorful ceramic cups.

ZESTY DRESSING:

⅓ cup mayonnaise
3 tablespoons buttermilk
I tablespoon honey mustard
2 teaspoons lemon juice
I tablespoon sugar
½ teaspoon lemon zest
½ teaspoon Tabasco

Mix all ingredients thoroughly. Refrigerate at least I hour or overnight.

SALAD:

I ½ cups fresh or frozen lima beans
I ½ cups fresh or frozen corn kernels
2 green onions, thinly sliced
I (7.5-ounce) jar roasted red bell peppers, drained

Boil lima beans 5 minutes; drain and cool. Boil corn 2 minutes; drain; cool. Mix with onions and peppers in a bowl. Pour Zesty Dressing over and mix gently. Serves 6.

Colorful Summertime Salad

6 large tomatoes, peeled, sliced
1 green bell pepper, seeded, sliced
1 red onion, sliced
¾ cup cider vinegar
1½ teaspoons celery salt
½ teaspoon dry mustard
¼ cup cold water
⅓ cup sugar
1 teaspoon Cajun seasoning

Place sliced vegetables in a baking dish. Combine remaining ingredients in glass measure; microwave on HIGH 70 seconds; stir. Pour over vegetables and refrigerate, covered, at least 4 hours before serving. Serves 6–8.

Use small cookie cutters to cut bell peppers into fun shapes—stars, moons, clovers.

Marinated Veggie Salad

¼ cup vinegar
¾ cup oil
2 tablespoons coarsely grated onion
¾ cup sugar
1 teaspoon dry mustard
2 stalks broccoli, chopped
½ head cauliflower, chopped
3 ribs celery, chopped
6 large mushrooms, sliced
½ red bell pepper, chopped

Combine vinegar, oil, onion, sugar, and dry mustard in quart jar with lid; shake well. Combine vegetables in large bowl; toss with dressing. Chill, covered, for several hours or overnight. Serves 8–10.

93

Rainbow Three Bean Salad

This keeps several days . . . nice to have at-the-ready!

1 (15½-ounce) can kidney beans, drained
1 (15-ounce) can waxed beans, drained
1 (15-ounce) can green beans, drained
1 green bell pepper, diced
1 purple onion, diced
1 stalk celery, diced
2 cups sugar
1 cup vinegar

Combine beans, pepper, onion, and celery in large bowl with cover. Heat sugar and vinegar until sugar is dissolved; mix well. Pour over vegetables; cover and refrigerate overnight. Serves 8 or more.

Summertime Tomato & Watermelon Salad

A refreshing summertime treat.

5 cups seeded watermelon, cut into ¾-inch cubes
2 tomatoes, cut into ¾-inch cubes
1 tablespoon sugar
½ teaspoon salt
1 small red onion, quartered, thinly sliced
½ cup red wine vinegar
¼ cup oil
Chilled lettuce leaves
Cracked black pepper to taste

Toss watermelon, tomatoes, sugar, and salt gently in large bowl. Let stand 15 minutes; drain. Stir in onion, vinegar, and oil. Cover and chill. Serve on lettuce leaves. Sprinkle with cracked black pepper. Serves 6.

Beautiful Watermelon Salad

So pretty, so refreshing, so totally delicious.

4 cups crisp torn red-leaf lettuce
20 (2-inch) cubes or triangles watermelon, seeded, drained
2 Bartlett pears, peeled, cut bite-size
20 bite-size broccoli florets, blanched 3 minutes, cooled
2 tablespoons Honey-Roasted Almond Accents
I cup flavored croutons

Arrange lettuce on 4 luncheon plates. Place watermelon, pears, and broccoli florets among leaves. Sprinkle with almonds; drizzle with shaken Watermelon Dressing. Serves 4. *(See full-color photograph in second insert following page 128.)*

WATERMELON DRESSING:
¼ cup light olive oil
2 tablespoons apple cider vinegar
I tablespoon sugar
¼ teaspoon Cajun seasoning
I teaspoon mustard
½ teaspoon lemon zest

Combine in a jar and shake well.

Small seedless watermelons are available in many markets many months of the year. Peel and cut in chunks; place in covered bowl till ready to assemble salad. Drain, then place chunks on lettuce just before serving. (Use containers with a drain tray, if available.)

Tropical Waldorf

2 Red Delicious apples, chopped
1 (8-ounce) can pineapple chunks, drained
¼ cup chopped celery
⅓ cup flaked coconut (optional)
⅓ cup raisins
½ cup chopped pecans
1 cup mini marshmallows
⅓ cup mayonnaise

Combine in bowl with cover. Mix well. Cover and refrigerate until ready to serve. Serves 4–6.

Nutty Cranberry Apple Salad

Quick to make, yet looks very elegant.

8 cups torn leaf lettuce
2 unpeeled apples, cut into bite-size pieces
½ cup crumbled blue cheese
⅓ cup dried cranberries
¼ cup chopped walnuts, toasted

Toss all together in big salad bowl.

POPPYSEED DRESSING:
½ cup canola oil
¼ cup sugar
¼ cup red wine vinegar
½ teaspoon poppyseed

In a jar with a tight-fitting lid, combine all; shake well. Pour over salad just before serving; toss to coat. Serves 10–12.

Editor's Extra: Pears make a great alternative to apples when in season.

96

Peanutty Apple Salad

1 (20-ounce) can pineapple chunks
½ cup sugar
1 tablespoon flour
1½ tablespoons cider vinegar
1 egg, beaten
1 (8-ounce) carton frozen whipped topping
1 cup dry roasted peanuts
2 medium apples, peeled, chopped
2 cups mini marshmallows

Drain juice from pineapple into a saucepan. Whisk in sugar, flour, vinegar, and egg; boil till thickened, stirring constantly; cool. Add remaining ingredients to sauce, including pineapple. Refrigerate. Serves 8–10.

Editor's Extra: Fun to add Heath bits when cool!

Creamy Apple-Beet Salad

Nice to serve on lettuce . . . or on its own.

1 medium apple
1 (14½-ounce) can whole beets
⅓ cup sour cream
1 tablespoon finely chopped onion
1 teaspoon salad seasoning

Peel, core, and halve apple. Slice as thinly as possible. Slice beets thinly. Gently mix apple and beet slices with sour cream until thoroughly coated. Sprinkle onion and seasoning over top. Serves 4–6.

The beets we use for most salads are called table beets, but are also known as garden beets, blood turnips, or red beets. They're a good source of Vitamin C, and their tops, big on Vitamin A, are good in salads, too. The garden beet is closely related to swiss chard and the sugar beet.

Tangy Apple Nut Salad

½ cup coarsely chopped pecans or walnuts
¼ cup mayonnaise
2 tablespoons cider vinegar
1 tablespoon lemon juice
3 tablespoons horseradish
3 tablespoons sugar
⅔ cup whipping cream, chilled
3 ribs celery, chopped
2 Red Delicious apples, peeled, chopped
Salt and pepper to taste

Toast nuts in a single layer on baking sheet at 350° for 10 minutes or until browned. Cool. Combine mayonnaise, vinegar, lemon juice, horseradish, and sugar; mix well. Beat cream in mixer bowl to soft peaks. Fold in mayonnaise mixture. Add celery, apples, salt and pepper. Spoon into serving bowl and sprinkle with toasted nuts. Chill. Serves 4–6.

Classic Pineapple-Orange Salad

1 (3-ounce) box orange Jell-O
1 (8-ounce) container small-curd cottage cheese
1 (12-ounce) container frozen whipped topping, thawed
2 (11-ounce) cans Mandarin oranges, well drained
1 (8-ounce) can crushed pineapple, well drained
¾ cup coarsely chopped toasted pecans

Combine Jell-O, cottage cheese, and whipped topping, mixing well. Add oranges, pineapple, and nuts; mix well. Chill before serving. Serves 6–8.

Easy Ambrosia

1 (11-ounce) can Mandarin oranges, drained
1 (8-ounce) can pineapple chunks, drained
1 cup seedless red grape halves
1 cup miniature marshmallows
1 banana, sliced
¾ cup vanilla yogurt or sour cream
½ cup flaked coconut

Combine all in large bowl. Serves 6–8.

Fruit Salad with Cottage Cheese

A special sauce makes a simple salad even better!

FRUIT SAUCE:
½ cup preserves (peach, pineapple, plum)
1 tablespoon white vinegar
2 tablespoons apple juice

Mix together in a jar.

SALAD:
4 cups torn romaine lettuce
2 fresh peaches, peeled, sliced (or canned)
1 pear, peeled, sliced (or canned)
2 cups small-curd cottage cheese
Pinch of salt
4 maraschino cherries for garnish

Arrange lettuce on 4 salad plates. Spoke fruit on top of lettuce, alternating peaches and pears. Spoon cottage cheese in center. Drizzle with warmed Fruit Sauce. Garnish with cherries. Serves 4.

What's in a name? In ancient Greek mythology, the word "ambrosia" is the food of the gods, sometimes giving ageless immortality to whoever consumes it. Oh well . . . worth a try.

99

Summer Fruit Salad

2 cups small-curd cottage cheese
1 (6-ounce) container any flavor fruit yogurt
6 cups cut-up fruit, such as peaches, nectarines,
    pears, bananas, pineapple chunks, raspberries,
    strawberries, etc.
½ cup chopped pecans
Lettuce leaves

Combine cottage cheese and yogurt in bowl; mix well. Arrange cut-up fruit and pecans on 6 lettuce-lined plates, and spoon ½ cup cottage cheese mixture on top. Serves 6.

Whatevahyagot Fruit Salad

Pear, apple, banana, and orange, some strawberries, grapes, cherries, dried cranberries, raisins . . . whatever you've got!

1–2 teaspoons lemon juice
4 cups cut, peeled fruit
1 heaping tablespoon mayonnaise
1 heaping tablespoon bottled ranch dressing

Squeeze lemon juice over cut fruit and toss. Add mayo and dressing; stir together gently. Serves 4. Will keep a day covered in the refrigerator.

Party Summer Salad

This serves a whole bunch of people . . . deliciously.

SUMMER SALAD DRESSING:

1 (8-ounce) package cream cheese, softened
½ cup frozen limeade or lemonade concentrate
⅓ cup powdered sugar
½ (8-ounce) carton Cool Whip

With mixer, beat cream cheese, concentrate, and powdered sugar on medium-high 3 minutes or until smooth. Fold in Cool Whip.

FRUITS:

2 cups cut-up honeydew melon
2 cups blueberries
2 ripe medium mangoes, peeled, cut up
1 quart strawberries, quartered
3 cups cut-up cantaloupe
Mint leaves

Layer honeydew melon, blueberries, and mangoes in trifle bowl. Spread half the Summer Salad Dressing over. Continue to layer strawberries and cantaloupe; spread remaining Dressing mixture on top. Garnish with mint leaves. Serves 20 or more.

Put dips and spreads and creamy salad dressings in edible fruit or "veggie bowls." Hollow out bell peppers, tomatoes, cabbages . . . you can even use leafy lettuce or endive cups.

Rainbow Melon Salad

SALAD:

⅔ **head romaine lettuce, torn (about 8 cups)**
1 cup cubed cantaloupe
1 cup cubed honeydew melon
1 cup halved strawberries

Combine all ingredients in large serving bowl; toss to mix. Pour Rainbow Vinaigrette over and toss to coat. Serves 10.

RAINBOW VINAIGRETTE:

2 tablespoons white wine vinegar
¼ **cup orange juice**
2 green onions, chopped
⅓ **cup sugar**
¼ **teaspoon salt**
⅓ **cup oil**
2 teaspoons poppyseed

Combine vinegar, orange juice, onions, sugar, and salt in food processor. With machine running, slowly add oil, blending until smooth. Add poppyseed; blend a few seconds to mix.

Grapefruit and Avocado Salad

An appetizing combination.

3 cups mixed salad greens
1 large grapefruit, peeled, sectioned
1 ripe avocado, peeled, pitted, sliced
¼ **large Vidalia onion, sliced, separated into thin rings**
Poppyseed dressing

Arrange salad greens on plate with grapefruit and avocado, arranged spoke-style; place onions on top. Drizzle with dressing. Serves 4–5.

Overnight Cherry Whip Salad

This is just as good served as a dessert. Superb!

2 large eggs
2 tablespoons sugar
1 cup heavy cream, divided
2 tablespoons lemon juice
2 cups frozen sour cherries, drained (do not substitute canned cherries)
1 (20-ounce) can pineapple tidbits, drained
2 (14½-ounce) cans Mandarin oranges, drained
1½ cups mini marshmallows
⅓ cup sliced almonds, chopped

Whisk eggs and sugar in a medium heat-proof bowl, and set bowl over a saucepan of simmering water. Whisk in ¼ cup heavy cream and the lemon juice; cook, whisking constantly, until mixture thickens slightly, about 5 minutes. Let cool completely.

Meanwhile, beat remaining ¾ cup heavy cream in mixer to soft peaks. Fold into cooled egg mixture.

Toss remaining ingredients in a large bowl. Pour cream mixture over, toss gently. Refrigerate at least 24 hours and up to 2 days. Serves 8–10.

The pineapple is one of the most delicious, popular fruits there is. But with its spiny armored outside, it doesn't even look like a fruit . . . it looks more like a pine cone, and that's where the name came from. Its Latin name is "ananas," a South American Indian word meaning "excellent fruit"—and that it is!

Bananas were first imported to the United States. in 1870, and just 28 years later, Americans in the United States were consuming over 16 million bunches a year. In 1876, at the Philadelphia Centennial Exhibition, Americans got their first "official" taste of bananas . . . they were wrapped in foil and sold for 10 cents.

Once bananas get ripe, store them in the refrigerator— the peels will darken, but the fruit stays pretty much the same for up to a week.

Mixed Berry Salad

2 bananas
A squeeze of lemon juice
4 cups spring mix greens
1 cup blackberries or raspberries (save 4 for top)
4 large strawberries, cut
$2/3$ cup blueberries
$1/3$ cup poppyseed dressing
4 dollops vanilla yogurt (or sour cream or mayonnaise)

Slice bananas into flat bowl and sprinkle with lemon (or pineapple) juice. On 4 salad plates, divide greens and arrange fruit around. Drizzle with poppyseed dressing and dollop yogurt or sour cream or mayonnaise in center. Garnish with a whole berry on top. Serves 4.

Black Cherry Salad

1 (6-ounce) package black cherry Jell-O
2 cups boiling water
1 (15-ounce) can pitted black cherries
1 (20-ounce) can crushed pineapple
$1/2$ cup chopped nuts

Dissolve Jell-O in boiling water; add fruits with juices and nuts and refrigerate until firm.

TOPPING:
1 (8-ounce) package cream cheese, softened
1 cup sour cream
$1/2$ cup sugar
$1/2$ teaspoon vanilla

Mix all and beat until blended. Spread on set Jell-O. Serves 8–10.

Strawberry Pretzel Salad

This salad would surely be voted most likely to "also serve as a dessert." Delicious.

2 cups crushed pretzels
3 tablespoons sugar
¾ cup butter, melted
1 (8-ounce) package cream cheese, softened
1 cup confectioners' sugar
1½ cups Cool Whip
2 (3-ounce) packages strawberry Jell-O
2 cups boiling water
2 (10-ounce) packages frozen strawberries

Mix pretzels with sugar and butter. Press into a 9x13-inch pan; bake at 375° for 8 minutes. Set aside. Cream cheese and confectioners' sugar; fold in Cool Whip. Spread over cooled crust.

Dissolve Jell-O in water and stir in strawberries; break up with fork. Chill till thickened (20 minutes or so). Spread over cream layer; chill. Serve with dollop of Cool Whip on cut squares. Serves 20–24.

Editor's Extra: Fun to add a cup of mini marshmallows or a small can of drained, crushed pineapple to the cream cheese mixture for variation.

The Dole Pineapple Plantation in Oahu started in 1950 as a fruit stand. It opened to the public as Hawaii's "Pineapple Experience" in 1989. Today it has many popular attractions, including the Plantation Express train, the Plantation Garden Tour, and the Pineapple Garden Maze (which is the world's largest). It welcomes more than a million visitors a year.

Hello Jell-O Salad

1 (16-ounce) carton small curd cottage cheese
1 (12-ounce) carton whipped topping
1 (20-ounce) can crushed pineapple, drained
1 (3-ounce) box Jell-O (any flavor)
½ cup chopped pecans or walnuts

Stir cottage cheese and whipped topping together; add pineapple. Sprinkle Jell-O over and stir together easily till mixed; fold in nuts. Refrigerate. Serves 12–16.

Nutty Lime Jell-O Salad

Pretty to serve in wine glasses with a dollop of cool whip and a cherry on top.

1 (3-ounce) package lime Jell-O
1¼ cups hot water
⅔ cup chopped pecans
⅓ (10½-ounce) bag mini marshmallows
1 (8-ounce) can crushed pineapple, undrained
¾ cup sour cream

Mix Jell-O and water; stir till dissolved. In another bowl, combine remaining ingredients; stir in Jell-O. Pour into ring mold and refrigerate. Serves 6–8.

Shrimp Pasta Salad

1 cup zesty Italian dressing
1 teaspoon dried basil
1 garlic clove, minced
1 tablespoon capers
$\frac{1}{8}$ teaspoon crushed red pepper
1½ cups rotini pasta, cooked, cooled
½ pound medium shrimp, cooked, peeled
1 cup halved grape tomatoes
¾ cup pimento-stuffed olives
⅓ cup chopped green bell pepper
3 cups torn salad greens
Feta cheese, crumbled (optional)

Whisk together salad dressing with basil, garlic, capers, and red pepper. Pour over pasta, shrimp, tomatoes, olives, and green pepper; toss. Divide salad greens onto 4–6 plates and spoon pasta mixture over greens. Sprinkle feta on top, if desired. Serves 4–6.

Overnight Chicken Pasta Salad

1 cup mayonnaise
1 cup sour cream
1 envelope ranch salad dressing mix
2 cups chopped cooked chicken
2 teaspoons lemon juice
1 teaspoon Greek seasoning
3 cups shredded lettuce
1 (8-ounce) can sliced water chestnuts, drained
1 cup tiny green peas
1 cup shell macaroni, cooked
1½ cups shredded Cheddar cheese
3 hard-boiled eggs, chopped

Mix first 3 ingredients in small bowl. In a large bowl, layer remaining ingredients in order listed. Put dressing mix on top, sealing to edge. Chill overnight. Before serving, toss gently. Serves 6–8.

Make-Ahead Chicken Penne Salad

HONEY-THYME DRESSING:

3 tablespoons oil
1 teaspoon crushed dried thyme leaves
1 ¼ cups mayonnaise
1 tablespoon milk
1 tablespoon honey
1 tablespoon coarse-grained mustard
1 teaspoon salt

Mix together; refrigerate.

SALAD:

1 (10-ounce) package penne pasta, cooked, drained
1 rotisserie chicken, skinned, cubed
2 stalks celery, sliced
2 cups halved red grapes
¼ cup chopped onion
1 cup chopped toasted walnuts, divided

Combine pasta, chicken, celery, grapes, and onion in salad bowl. Toss with Honey-Thyme Dressing 1–2 hours before serving. Cover and refrigerate. Just before serving, stir in most of walnuts, saving some to sprinkle on top. Serves 8.

Pasta Garden Salad

DILL DRESSING:

1 cup mayonnaise
1 green onion, chopped
1 tablespoon lemon juice
1 teaspoon dried dill
½ teaspoon salt
½ teaspoon lemon pepper

Mix ingredients until smooth.

SALAD:

4 ounces spaghetti, quartered, cooked
1 small cucumber, seeded, chopped
1 carrot, thinly sliced
1 zucchini, thinly sliced
4 radishes, thinly sliced
¼ green bell pepper, chopped

Toss Salad with Dill Dressing in large bowl; cover and chill. Serves 8–10.

Tomato Basil Pasta Salad

2½ cups uncooked shell macaroni
1 bundle fresh asparagus spears, trimmed, cut
1 pint grape tomatoes, cut in half
¾ cup chopped bell pepper
1 (8-ounce) bottle tomato and basil salad
   dressing

Boil pasta 7 minutes in plenty of water. Add asparagus and boil 3 minutes more; drain. Rinse with cold water; drain. Pour mixture into large salad bowl with tomatoes and bell pepper. Add dressing; toss gently. Serves 6–10.

The record for the largest salad is 14,991.4 pounds and was achieved by the town of Pulpi, Spain, at the Pulpi fairground, in Pulpi, Almeria (Spain), on September 27, 2007. It had lettuces, cherry tomatoes, olives, bell pepper slices, etc., etc., etc. Now that's a big salad!

Florida Rice Salad

4 cups cooked brown and wild rice
½ cup sliced green onions
½ cup golden raisins
½ cup chopped walnuts
½ cup frozen orange juice concentrate, thawed, undiluted
1 tablespoon olive oil
Salt and pepper to taste

Mix rice, onions, raisins, and nuts in large bowl. Whisk remaining ingredients; stir with rice mixture; chill. Serves 6–8.

Ham 'n Cheese Rice Salad

MUSTARD DRESSING:
½ cup sour cream
⅓ cup mayonnaise or salad dressing
2 tablespoons spicy brown mustard

Combine ingredients; blend well.

SALAD:
2 cups diced ham
1 cup diced provolone cheese
½ cup chopped celery
2 cups cooked white rice, chilled
4 cups torn romaine lettuce

Mix all ingredients except lettuce. Pour Mustard Dressing over and toss to coat. Divide lettuce onto 6 plates; spoon rice mixture on lettuce. Serves 6.

Really Nice Rice Salad

so good . . . and good for you.

3 cups cooked brown rice
¾ cup frozen peas, thawed
1 (4-ounce) can sliced ripe olives
4 green onions, sliced
10 cherry tomatoes, quartered
¼ cup snipped fresh basil
⅓ cup toasted pine nuts
¼ cup olive oil
1½ tablespoons balsamic vinegar
½ teaspoon Greek seasoning

In large bowl, combine rice, peas, olives, onions, tomatoes, basil, and nuts. Add oil, vinegar, and seasoning; toss. Serves 4–6.

Editor's Extra: Any rice will do for this salad, as well as bulgur wheat or acini di pepe pasta.

white rice has the hull and bran removed, but in the United States is generally enriched with nutrients. Brown rice has just the hull removed, so has more fiber and nutrition. Converted rice is boiled or steamed before it is processed, forcing some vitamins and minerals into the kernel from the bran, so is higher in nutrients than plain white rice. And wild rice is not a grain, but a seed of a grass.

Mandarin Wild Rice Salad

The sesame dressing adds just the right touch.

SALAD:

3 cups cooked wild and long-grain rice
2 cups chunked cooked chicken
1 cup fresh snow pea pods, cut in thirds
1 (11-ounce) can Mandarin oranges, drained

While rice is cooking, mix chicken, pea pods, and oranges together. Refrigerate.

When rice is cooled, toss with Salad. Add Sesame Dressing and toss again. Cover and refrigerate till ready to serve. Serves 4–6.

SESAME DRESSING:

¼ cup oil
3 tablespoons cider vinegar
3 tablespoons soy sauce
2 tablespoons sugar
1 tablespoon parsley flakes
2 tablespoons toasted sesame seeds
½ teaspoon ginger
¼ teaspoon pepper

Combine all in a jar with a tight-fitting lid. Shake well; refrigerate.

Meat and Seafood Salads

Catalina Chicken Salad

¾ pound chicken tenders, cut into strips
1 cup Catalina dressing, divided
1 (10-ounce) package salad greens
10–12 strawberries, sliced
¼ cup sliced almonds

Cook chicken in $\frac{1}{4}$ of the dressing in medium skillet on medium heat 8–10 minutes till cooked; cool slightly. Toss with greens, strawberries, and almonds in a salad bowl. Drizzle with remaining dressing and toss again. Serves 4.

Chicken Salad in Tomato Flowers

A photo finish salad.

2 cups chicken salad (bought or homemade)
10 seedless red or green grapes, quartered
⅓ cup coarsely chopped pecans, toasted
1 teaspoon Dijon mustard
¼ teaspoon curry powder
Lettuce leaves
4 medium-firm tomatoes
Parsley sprigs for garnish

Mix chicken salad with grapes, nuts, mustard, and curry powder. Arrange lettuce on salad plates. Cut each tomato into 6 wedges, cutting to, but not through bottom. Open each "flower" and spoon $\frac{1}{2}$ cup chicken salad in center. Garnish with parsley. Serves 4. *(See full-color photograph in second insert following page 128.)*

store cleaned, long-stemmed herbs such as parsley, cilantro, and dill in a tall glass with stem ends down. Fill with about an inch of cold water. cover leaves with a plastic bag and refrigerate until ready to use. change water every two or three days and herbs should stay fresh for about five days.

113

Is it a salad? or a sandwich? chicken and tuna salad, and any such kind of salad that has a moisture ingredient to hold it together can be both. If you stuff it in a pita pocket, or roll it in a tortilla and can pick it up with your hands to bite it, then it's more like a sandwich. If it's piled on lettuce on a plate and you need a fork . . . then it must be a salad.

Nutty Chicken Salad

1 (16-ounce) package mixed salad greens
2 cups sliced grilled chicken
½ cup walnut pieces
½ carton fresh raspberries
¾ cup raspberry vinaigrette

Place greens in large bowl or divide onto individual plates. Top with chicken, nuts, and berries. Drizzle with dressing. Serves 6.

Strawberry-Pecan Chicken Salad

A quick salad with an exotic dressing, but good with poppyseed dressing right out of the bottle, too!

GINGERY DRESSING:
½ cup mayonnaise
¼ cup lemon yogurt
½ teaspoon sugar
¼ teaspoon ground ginger
Dash of salt and pepper

SALAD:
3 cups chopped rotisserie chicken, skinned
¾ cup chopped celery
½ cup chopped pecans
1 cup wedged strawberries
Bibb lettuce

Toss all but lettuce in salad bowl with Gingery Dressing. Serve on lettuce leaves. Serves 4–6.

Editor's Extra: Make this into a delicious, elegant sandwich, by stuffing salad into a warm croissant.

Margarita Salad

A lovely dinner salad.

1 tablespoon vinegar
6 tablespoons frozen margarita mix, thawed
6 cups torn salad greens
1 (6-ounce) package cooked southwest-flavored
  chicken strips
1 (11-ounce) can Mandarin oranges, drained
2 avocados, peeled, pitted, sliced
Lime wedges

Combine vinegar and margarita mix; mix well. Arrange salad greens on serving platter. Top with chicken, oranges, and avocados. Pour margarita mixture over salad. Garnish with lime wedges. Serves 4–6.

Though one cup per serving is a general rule of thumb, it is a guess to determine how many servings a given salad recipe will make, as it could be a before-dinner salad or the meal itself. Best to take "serves 4-6" with a grain of salt.

Light Taos Chicken Salad

This is a delightful "meal salad" that's easy on the calories.

½ cup light ranch salad dressing
¼ cup salsa
Dash of ground cumin
1 (10-ounce) package salad greens
1 (6-ounce) package cooked southwest-flavored
  chicken strips, cut small
1 medium tomato, diced
4 green onions, sliced
1 avocado, peeled, sliced
½ cup reduced-fat Mexican-style cheese
Tortilla strips for garnish

In a large serving bowl, mix ranch dressing, salsa, and cumin. Add salad greens, chopped chicken strips, tomato, and green onions. Toss to coat with dressing.

To serve, arrange tossed salad on serving plate; top with avocado, cheese, and tortilla strips. Serves 4–6.

Editor's Extra: You can buy packaged tortilla strips in the produce section.

CHICKEN FOR SALADS
- Buy ready-cooked chicken.
- Use leftover chicken.
- Use a rotisserie cooked chicken and bone it.
- Microwave boneless chicken breasts cut into chunks. Add 1/2 cup broth. Cook covered on HIGH 4 minutes.
- Boil boneless chicken breasts covered in broth; boil, then simmer 10 minutes.
- Pan sauté boneless chicken breasts cut into chunks in small amount of oil or butter for 10 minutes.
- Oven-bake chunks of chicken in seasoned water or broth at 400° for 20-25 minutes till cooked.
- Dry bake Pam-sprayed chunks on Pam-sprayed baking pan 15-20 minutes at 400°.

Greek Salad of the Gods

SALAD:
8 cups torn romaine lettuce
2 cups thinly sliced rotisserie chicken, skinned
1 ½ cups halved cherry tomatoes
1 small cucumber, sliced
½ cup halved pitted kalamata olives
4 thin slices red onion, separated
⅓ cup crumbled feta cheese

Toss all ingredients except feta cheese. Pour Greek Dressing over and toss again. Arrange Salad on serving plates and sprinkle with cheese. Serves 6.

GREEK DRESSING:
¾ cup Italian salad dressing
1 tablespoon lemon juice
1 teaspoon dried dill weed
¼ teaspoon Greek seasoning

Combine ingredients well; pour over Salad and toss to coat.

Chicken, Cherry, Cheese Salad

6 cups fresh baby spinach leaves
2 cups chopped rotisserie chicken, skinned
1 (16-ounce) can Bing cherries, pitted, halved
½ cup crumbled Gorgonzola cheese
2 tablespoons chopped green onions
½ cup poppyseed or Italian dressing (or combo)

Arrange spinach leaves on 6 salad plates; divide chicken, cherries, cheese, and onions evenly over spinach. Drizzle with dressing. Serves 6.

Tall Tex Taco Salad

TALL TEX DRESSING:
1/4 cup white vinegar
2 tablespoons vegetable oil
2 tablespoons sugar
1/2 teaspoon salt
1/2 teaspoon ground cumin

Shake ingredients in jar.

SALAD:
6 cups torn lettuce
2 medium tomatoes, wedged thinly
1 chicken, cooked, deboned, chopped
2 tablespoons finely chopped onion
1 (4-ounce) can chopped green chiles, drained
Tortilla chips
1/2 cup shredded taco-flavored Cheddar cheese

Toss all together but chips and cheese. Add dressing; toss again. Edge platter or individual serving plates with tortilla chips and pile Salad in the middle; sprinkle with cheese Serves 6.

Big Island Chicken Salad

1 (10-ounce) bag baby spinach leaves
1 (10-ounce) bag spring mix lettuce
1 cup fresh pineapple chunks or 1 (8-ounce) can, drained
1 cup chopped red bell pepper
3 tablespoons chopped green onions
2 cups chopped rotisserie chicken, skinned
1/3 cup Italian dressing
3 tablespoons orange marmalade
2 tablespoons sliced almonds

Toss spinach and spring mix; top with pineapple, bell pepper, onions, and chicken. In a bowl, stir Italian dressing with orange marmalade. Drizzle over salad. Sprinkle with almonds. Serves 6–8, or 4 as a main-course salad.

Overnight Pepperoni Chicken Salad

The dressing has a bit of a nip that makes it pizzazzy!

1 (10-ounce) bag bite-size salad greens
1 ½ cups chopped cooked chicken
½ small red onion, thinly sliced into rings
1 zucchini, thinly sliced
¾ cup shredded Monterey Jack cheese
⅔ cup chopped pepperoni
2 cups halved cherry tomatoes
1 cup mayonnaise
1 tablespoon mustard
½ teaspoon horseradish

Place half the lettuce in a glass bowl. Layer with chicken, onion, zucchini, cheese, pepperoni, remaining lettuce, and tomatoes.

In a small bowl, mix mayonnaise, mustard, and horseradish. Spread over salad to edge of bowl. Cover and refrigerate up to 24 hours. Garnish with additional cherry tomatoes and parsley, if desired. Serves 8.

Southwest Chicken Caesar Salad

1 (10-ounce) package romaine salad greens
1 (1-pound) package southwest-flavored grilled chicken strips
1 cup seasoned croutons
½ cup grated Parmesan cheese
¾ cup Caesar Italian dressing

Toss lettuce, chicken, croutons, and cheese with dressing in large bowl. Serve with fresh lemon wedges and freshly ground pepper, if desired. Serves 4.

Fruity Chicken Salad

1 apple, peeled, chopped
1 (15-ounce) can pineapple tidbits
1 cup seedless grapes, halved
3 cups chopped cooked chicken
Lettuce
$\frac{1}{3}$ cup toasted sliced almonds

Put apple in bowl; drain pineapple over apples; wait 2 minutes, then drain apples, saving juice. Add pineapple chunks, grapes, and chicken. Toss lightly with Creamy Dressing. Serve on lettuce; sprinkle with almonds. Serves 6–8.

CREAMY DRESSING:
2 tablespoons butter
3 tablespoons sugar
1 tablespoon cornstarch
Juice of 1 lemon
$\frac{1}{4}$ cup reserved pineapple juice
$\frac{1}{2}$ cup whipping cream, whipped

Heat all but whipped cream in saucepan a few minutes till smooth. Cool slightly then fold in whipped cream.

Metal knives cause lettuce to turn brown where cut; a plastic knife will not. When using a knife to shred lettuce to be used right away, be sure the knife is sharp, cut lettuce in half, and place cut side down on cutting board. Cut across the halves into thin slices, then separate slices into shreds.

Supreme Chicken Salad

This will become a favorite.

2 cups cooked chopped chicken
1 cup halved seedless grapes
$\frac{1}{2}$ cup slivered almonds
$\frac{3}{4}$ cup diced celery
1 cup mayonnaise
$\frac{1}{2}$ teaspoon curry powder
1 tablespoon lemon juice

Mix all together; serve on lettuce leaves or pineapple slices. Top with additional slivered almonds, if desired. Serves 4.

Asian Chicken and Bean Salad

ASIAN DRESSING:
$\frac{1}{3}$ **cup mayonnaise**
1 $\frac{1}{2}$ teaspoons grated fresh gingerroot
1 tablespoon soy sauce
2 teaspoons red wine vinegar
$\frac{1}{4}$ teaspoon prepared mustard
1 garlic clove, minced

Mix all in small bowl or jar.

1 (15-ounce) can red kidney beans, drained
2 cups shredded cooked chicken or cooked
** chicken strips**
$\frac{1}{2}$ cup chopped seeded cucumber
$\frac{1}{4}$ cup sliced green onions
Lettuce leaves

Combine all in large bowl; mix well. Spoon Asian Dressing over chicken mixture; toss gently until well coated. Serve immediately, or cover and refrigerate until serving time. Serve on lettuce-lined plates. Serves 4.

Editor's Extra: You may substitute your favorite canned beans for kidney beans (black, pinto, Great Northern).

Turkey Waldorf Salad

2 medium red apples, chopped
1 ½ cups cubed cooked turkey
½ cup chopped celery
¼ cup raisins
⅓ cup mayonnaise or salad dressing
1 tablespoon lemon juice
4 cups torn butter lettuce
¼ cup chopped toasted walnuts

Combine apples, turkey, celery, raisins, mayonnaise, and lemon juice; mix well. Arrange lettuce on salad plates; spoon apple mixture onto lettuce; sprinkle with walnuts. Serves 4–6.

Editor's Extra: Make this a traditional Waldorf Salad by eliminating turkey. Good to sub dried cranberries for raisins, and pecans for walnuts.

Turkey in the Orchard Salad

PEACH DRESSING:
¼ cup oil
¼ cup peach preserves
2 tablespoons vinegar

Process or blend all ingredients till smooth.

SALAD:
2 cups cubed smoked or cooked turkey
3 medium fresh peaches or nectarines, peeled, thinly sliced
1 pint fresh strawberries, halved
6 cups torn mixed salad greens
½ cup pecan halves, toasted

Combine turkey, peaches, strawberries, and greens in large bowl. Pour Peach Dressing over Salad; toss to coat. Top with pecan halves. Serves 6.

Editor's Extra: You can sometimes find rotisserie turkey breasts "under the lights" at your supermarket.

A waldorf salad consists of julienned apple and celery, chopped walnuts and grapes, with a mayonnaise or a mayonnaise-based dressing. The salad was first created around 1893 at the Waldorf Hotel in New York city ... which in 1931 became the Waldorf-Astoria Hotel. The maitre d'hotel Oscar Tschirky is usually given credit for creating the recipe (and he also claims credit for Eggs Benedict). But some claim it was created by the Waldorf Lunch System, an early 20th-century lunch-room chain whose logo was an apple.

Mighty Meaty Chef's Salad

1 (10-ounce) package mixed salad greens
½ pound sliced cooked ham or roast beef, cut in
  strips
1 cup sliced fresh mushrooms
1 cup halved cherry tomatoes
½ cup crumbled blue cheese
¾ cup balsamic vinaigrette

In large serving bowl, layer salad greens, meat, mushrooms, tomatoes, and cheese. Pour vinaigrette over salad just before serving. Serves 6.

Ribbon Nest Pork Salad

1 pound boneless pork loin, cut into cubes
2 tablespoons orange juice
½ cup sweet and sour sauce, divided
4 cups shredded napa cabbage
1 small zucchini, cut into thin ribbons
1 small yellow summer squash, cut into thin ribbons
1 cup chow mein noodles

Cook pork in a nonstick skillet for 5 minutes. Add juice and ¼ cup sweet and sour sauce; heat until bubbly, stirring frequently until pork is cooked and glazed. Remove skillet from heat.

Arrange cabbage on serving platter. Top with zucchini and squash ribbons and pork. Sprinkle with noodles; drizzle with remaining ¼ cup sweet and sour sauce. Serves 4.

Hearty Bean and Beef Salad

1 (15½-ounce) can red kidney beans, rinsed, drained
1½ cups cooked roast beef, cut into short strips
1¼ cups frozen corn kernels, thawed
1 cup sliced celery
¼ cup chopped sweet onion
Lettuce leaves

Combine beans, beef, corn, celery, and onion. Toss with Orange Honey Mustard Dressing. Serve over lettuce leaves. Serves 4–6.

ORANGE HONEY MUSTARD DRESSING:
2 tablespoons orange juice
¼ cup Dijon mustard
1 tablespoon mayonnaise
1 tablespoon honey
⅓ cup plain yogurt

Stir all together till smooth.

Steak Strip Meal Salad

1 pound beef sirloin steak
1½ cups Italian dressing, divided
½ pound new potatoes, quartered
1 (10-ounce) package mixed salad greens
16–20 grape tomatoes
½ cup thinly sliced red onion

Marinate steak in 1 cup dressing; cover and refrigerate 3 hours or overnight.

Drain steak; discard dressing. Place potatoes and steak in double layer of aluminum foil to form a pouch; top with remaining ½ cup dressing.

Grill steak and potato pouch over medium coals 15 minutes or till desired doneness (or broil in oven). Cut steak across grain into thin strips. Toss greens, tomatoes, onion, steak strips, and potatoes. Toss with additional dressing, if desired. Serves 4.

Be adventurous with fruits, nuts, unusual vegetables, and even meats to make a more interesting salad. Make it a main meal by adding grilled chicken or beef, broiled salmon or tuna, ham cubes, etc. Try vegetables other than the standard "salad vegetables," such as garbanzo or kidney beans, squash, corn, beets, and even sweet potato chunks. If it's edible, it can probably go on a salad!

Sirloin Beef Salad

Great use of leftover steak.

1 pound top sirloin, cut 1 inch thick
1½ teaspoons Cajun seasoning
1 red bell pepper, seeded, halved
1 onion, thickly sliced
1 (12-ounce) package torn romaine lettuce

Season steak with Cajun seasoning. Grill steak, red pepper, and onion 4–6 inches from medium coals, 12–15 minutes, turning once.

Slice steak diagonally into ¼-inch-thick strips. Slice pepper into thin strips. Arrange steak, peppers, and onion slices over lettuce. Serve with warm Bacon Dressing. Serves 4.

BACON DRESSING:
3–4 strips bacon, fried crisp, crumbled, reserve
**   drippings**
1 tablespoon flour
½ cup water
½ cup vinegar
2 tablespoons sugar
Salt and pepper to taste

Blend bacon drippings with flour in skillet; add water, vinegar, and sugar; stir constantly. Cook till thickened; salt and pepper to taste; add crumbled bacon.

Fruit Salad over Grilled Steak

Nice when you have leftover beef or chicken.

THE FRUIT:

1 (11-ounce) can Mandarin oranges, drained
3 plums, peeled, cut bite size
1 tablespoon chopped fresh mint
¼ cup frozen orange juice concentrate, thawed
2 tablespoons white wine vinegar
1 tablespoon oil

Combine all; cover and refrigerate.

THE SALAD:

¼ cup brown sugar
2 teaspoons Italian seasoning mix
2 teaspoons minced garlic
¾ pound beef flank steak
6 cups torn salad greens

Combine brown sugar, seasoning, and garlic; mix well and rub on steak; let stand at room temperature 15 minutes. Grill over medium heat 12–15 minutes to medium doneness, turning once. Cut steak diagonally across grain into very thin slices. Place salad greens on 6 serving plates; top with steak slices and fruit mixture. Serves 6.

Wash greens in cold water and spin in lettuce spinner, or pat dry with paper towels. Store greens wrapped between dry paper towels, if desired, in a perforated plastic bag, or loosely wrapped in plastic bag in refrigerator.

Leafy Taco Salad

A fiesta on a plate!

1 pound lean ground beef
⅔ cup water
1 (1½-ounce) package taco seasoning
1 head romaine or iceberg lettuce, torn
1 (15-ounce) can pinto beans, drained, rinsed
2 tomatoes, chopped
5 green onions, sliced
1 cup shredded sharp Cheddar cheese
1 cup salsa
1 cup sour cream
Tortilla chips

Brown beef over medium-high heat; drain. Stir in water and taco seasoning; turn heat to medium-low. Cook another few minutes until most liquid has evaporated.

Arrange lettuce on 6–8 salad plates. Add a scoop of meat mixture, then remaining ingredients, putting chips around salad. Serves 6–8.

West Indies Crab Salad

1 pound lump crabmeat
1 medium sweet onion, chopped
½ cup seasoned rice wine vinegar
⅓ cup oil
Salt and pepper to taste
5 ice cubes
4 cups torn lettuce

Put crabmeat in a bowl with a lid; put onion on top of crabmeat. Combine vinegar and oil and pour over crabmeat and onion. Season to taste. Put ice cubes on top. Do NOT stir. Chill 12 hours, covered. Serve with slotted spoon on a bed of lettuce. Serves 4 or 5.

Crab Louie Salad

1 head iceberg lettuce, chopped
8–12 ounces cooked lump crabmeat
1 avocado, peeled, pitted, wedged
3 tomatoes, wedged
½ cup chopped black olives
2 hard-boiled eggs, chopped

On a large plate or platter, make a bed of iceberg lettuce. Top with remaining ingredients. Drizzle with Louie Dressing. Serves 4–6.

LOUIE DRESSING:
1 cup mayonnaise
½ cup chili sauce
¼ cup minced scallions
1 teaspoon fresh lemon juice
1 teaspoon bottled horseradish

Mix all together in a jar.

Editor's Extra: Good idea to squeeze a little lemon juice over the avocado slices if not serving immediately.

Crab Louie (or crab Louis) salad is also known as the "King of Salads" and features crabmeat, preferably Dungeness. It originated on the West Coast and dates back to the early 1700's.

Sautéed Shrimp over Tender Greens

⅓ cup olive oil
12–16 medium shrimp, peeled, deveined
¼ cup balsamic vinegar
⅓ cup dry white wine
½ teaspoon Greek seasoning
1 (10-ounce) bag spring mix

Place oil in skillet over medium-high heat. Add shrimp, tossing to coat. Sauté until lightly colored, 1–2 minutes. Add vinegar, wine, and seasoning, and cook until liquid is reduced, about 2 minutes.

Arrange salad greens on 4 plates; place shrimp over greens, and spoon any remaining liquid over all. Serve at once. Serves 4.

A question of aesthetics! While it isn't necessary, some people say shrimp look and taste better when deveined. Most cooks won't bother deveining small and medium shrimp. But since you can see the vein through the meat, it's better to devein shrimp for salads.

Shrimp 'n Melon Salad

6 cups torn romaine lettuce
1 pound cooked medium shrimp
2 cups bite-size cantaloupe
3 cups bite-size honeydew melon
1 cup bottled honey Dijon salad dressing

Arrange romaine lettuce on serving platter. Scatter shrimp, cantaloupe, and honeydew melon on top. Drizzle salad dressing over all. Serves 6.

Caribbean Mango Shrimp Salad

SALAD:
4 cups torn mixed greens
1 pound cooked, peeled, deveined medium shrimp
2 ripe mangoes, peeled, seeded, chopped
1 small cucumber, peeled, cubed
½ medium red bell pepper, chopped
1 fresh jalapeño chile, seeded, finely chopped
¼ cup toasted chopped macadamia nuts or almonds

Arrange salad greens on 4–6 salad plates. In a bowl, toss shrimp, mangoes, cucumber, pepper, and jalapeño; mix with Citrus Dressing; spoon onto salad greens. Sprinkle with nuts. Serves 4–6.

CITRUS DRESSING:
⅓ cup frozen limeade mix, thawed, undiluted
2 tablespoons orange marmalade
3 tablespoons vinegar
3 tablespoons vegetable oil

Blend all ingredients.

Muffuletta Salad (page 90)

Beautiful Watermelon Salad (page 95)

Tuna-Cone Salads (page 132)

Chicken Salad in Tomato Flowers (page 113)

Fit-For-A-King Chopped Salad

CANDIED CINNAMON PECANS:

⅓ cup sliced-lengthwise pecans

1 tablespoon dark brown sugar

½ teaspoon cinnamon

1½ teaspoons butter, melted

Toss all together well and bake on a parchment-lined baking sheet 5–8 minutes in 375° oven until sugar is caramelized; cool.

BLUE CHEESE VINAIGRETTE:

¼ cup olive oil

¼ cup white or champagne vinegar

¼ teaspoon balsamic vinegar

2 teaspoons Dijon mustard

2 tablespoons sour cream

2 tablespoons chopped fresh basil

Salt and freshly ground black pepper to taste

½ cup crumbled blue cheese

Whisk all together.

SALAD:

3 cups chopped iceberg lettuce

3 cups chopped Bibb or butter lettuce

3 cups chopped red leaf lettuce

1 green onion, sliced

36–40 shrimp, peeled, deveined, and grilled

Place chopped lettuces in a large serving bowl. Toss with vinaigrette thoroughly to coat. Sprinkle onion and pecans over salad. Add shrimp. Serves 8–10.

Editor's Extra: This salad is similar to those served at Outback and Ruth's Chris Steak House.

Salads fit for a king? The kings and queens of Europe were notably fond of salads. King Henry IV of England liked a bowl of sliced new potatoes and sardines with herb dressing. Mary, Queen of Scots, liked lettuce, boiled celery root, truffles, chervil, and hard-boiled eggs in a mustard dressing.

129

Grilled Salmon Salad

SALAD:

8 small red potatoes, cut into wedges
2 cups fresh green beans, cut
1 (1-pound) fresh salmon fillet
1 (10-ounce) package mixed salad greens
1 (4-ounce) can sliced ripe olives, drained
½ red onion, thinly sliced
Lemon wedges

In saucepan, boil potatoes and green beans in water to cover. Cook 10–15 minutes on medium heat or until potatoes and green beans are tender. Rinse with cold water; drain. Refrigerate until chilled.

Place salmon fillet, skin side down, on gas grill over medium heat; cover grill. Cook 12–15 minutes or until fish flakes easily with fork. Remove skin; break fish into pieces.

Place salad greens on salad plates. Arrange potatoes, green beans, salmon, olives, onion slices, and lemon wedges on greens. Serves 4.

DIJON VINAIGRETTE:

¼ cup white wine vinegar
½ cup light olive oil
1 teaspoon sugar
1 tablespoon Dijon mustard
1 teaspoon minced garlic

Blend all ingredients well. Drizzle over Salad.

oil and vinegar have been dressing greens and vegetables since Babylonian times, some 2,000 years ago. The word "salad" can be traced to the ancient Romans who sprinkled salt on grasses and herbs, calling it herba salata. Roman and Greek cooks later experimented with olive oil, vinegar, and salt, then added wine, honey, and fermented fish sauces known as garum. (Maybe that's how the anchovies found their way into Caesar's salad.)

Simon Says Sample Simple Salmon Salad

We had a lot of laughs over this title. Look away and try to say it . . . you'll laugh, too.

1 (1-pound) salmon fillet, grilled
½ cup Caesar salad dressing, divided
1 (10-ounce) bag torn romaine lettuce
½ cup flavored croutons
¼ cup sliced ripe olives
3 tablespoons shredded fresh Parmesan cheese

Brush salmon fillet with a tablespoon of Caesar dressing before grilling.

Toss lettuce, croutons, and olives; pour remaining dressing over top; toss gently to coat. Spoon salad onto large platter. Remove skin from salmon and flake. Arrange salmon on top of salad. Sprinkle with cheese.

Mose's Tuna Salad

2 (6-ounce) cans tuna, drained
2 hard-boiled eggs, diced
2 tablespoons sweet pickle relish
1 apple, peeled, diced
1 rib celery, finely diced
¼–½ teaspoon dried basil
½ teaspoon Greek seasoning
3–4 tablespoons mayonnaise

Combine all ingredients and mix well. Refrigerate for flavors to mingle. Serve on lettuce as salad, or on bread for sandwich. Serves 4.

Tuna-Cone Salads

4 (6-inch) flour tortillas
I cup torn lettuce
2 teaspoons Almond Accents (in salad section)
I (6-ounce) can tuna, drained
¼ Red Delicious apple, peeled (if desired), diced
½ stalk celery, diced
I ½ tablespoons mayonnaise
Salt and pepper to taste

On tortillas, divide lettuce on half of each; sprinkle with almonds. Mix remaining ingredients and spoon evenly on top; roll into cones. Wrap in wax paper, then foil. Good to go! Serves 4. *(See full-color photograph in second insert following page 128.)*

Pineapple Tuna Salad

Great on lettuce or for sandwiches.

I (6-ounce) can tuna, drained
½ cup plain yogurt
I (8-ounce) can crushed pineapple, drained
¼ cup sweet pickle relish
2 ribs celery, finely chopped
¼ cup chopped pecans
2 teaspoons yellow mustard

Mix all ingredients in bowl. Refrigerate till serving time. Serves 4.

Salad Dressings

Brown Derby's Cobb Salad Dressing

cobb salad is made of lettuce, tomatoes, bacon, chicken, hard-cooked eggs, avocado, chives, and roquefort cheese. The dressing makes it extra special.

¼ cup red wine vinegar
¼ cup water
¼ teaspoon sugar
I small clove garlic, finely minced
I teaspoon fresh lemon juice
¾ teaspoon Worcestershire
2 teaspoons salt
¾ teaspoon freshly ground black pepper
¼ teaspoon dry English mustard
¼ cup olive oil
¾ cup salad oil

Blend or process all ingredients except oils. Blend in oils. Just before drizzling on salads, blend again. Makes 1 ½ cups.

salad oil is a catch-all word for any vegetable oil. canola oil is made from a modified variant of rapeseed oil. olive oil comes from olives; peanut oil from peanuts, and all the other kinds come from their namesakes as well. so when you see salad oil called for in a recipe, know that it leaves the choice up to you.

Maria's Garlic Tomato Marinade

Mama Mia, Ms. Maria, that's I-tah-yun!

⅓ cup finely minced onion
5 baby toes garlic, finely minced
5 juicy tomatoes, chopped very small (save juice)
½ teaspoon Creole seasoning
I (8-ounce) bottle Italian salad dressing
Salt and pepper to taste

Combine all in a serving bowl, being sure to get all the juice from the tomatoes. Refrigerate an hour or more.

At serving time, put the bowl on the table along with a big bowl of crisp lettuce and let everybody serve themselves. Makes 4 cups.

Light Balsamic Vinaigrette

½ cup balsamic vinegar
2 tablespoons light olive oil
2 tablespoons water
1 tablespoon sugar
1 teaspoon Italian seasoning
⅛ teaspoon salt
1 clove garlic, minced

Mix all ingredients in a jar; refrigerate. Shake before using. Makes ¾ cup.

Vidalia Onion Vinaigrette

Serve this lively dressing over your favorite blend of salad greens.

1 Vidalia onion, quartered
⅓ cup red wine vinegar
¾ cup sugar
1 tablespoon dry mustard
1 teaspoon salt
1 cup vegetable or olive oil
1½ teaspoons poppyseed

Process onion in a food processor or blender until finely minced. Add vinegar, sugar, mustard, and salt; process until well-mixed. With processor running, add oil in a slow, steady stream. Stir in poppyseed. Makes 2⅔ cups.

Sun-Dried Tomato Vinaigrette

⅓ cup finely chopped sun-dried tomatoes
I teaspoon garlic powder
½ teaspoon oregano
¼ teaspoon black pepper
Salt to taste
2 tablespoons balsamic vinegar
⅓ cup olive oil

Let tomatoes and spices soak in vinegar for a couple of hours before adding oil. Makes ⅔ cup.

Raspberry Vinaigrette

½ cup wine vinegar
⅓ cup raspberry preserves
2 tablespoons sugar
I cup light olive oil

Whisk (or blend in blender) vinegar, preserves, and sugar. Add olive oil in thin stream, whisking (or blending) till well blended. Bottle and refrigerate. Shake before adding to salad greens. Makes about 2 cups.

Blender Basil Dressing

½ cup lightly packed fresh basil leaves
I cup mayonnaise
½ cup sour cream
½ cup chopped green onions
I teaspoon chopped garlic
¼ cup apple cider vinegar
½ teaspoon dry mustard
Salt and pepper to taste

Combine all ingredients in a blender until smooth. Makes 3 cups.

Basil is for lovers! An annual herb of the mint family, basil is native to Africa and India. In addition to its culinary uses, basil is also used in perfumes, soaps, shampoos, and dental preparations.

In Mexico, basil is supposed to keep a lover's eye off others, and is considered a powerful protector in Haiti. In Italy, it is a token of love. In Romania, if a girl gives a sprig to her boyfriend, they are engaged. A good Hindu goes to rest with a basil leaf on his breast as a passport to paradise.

The ratio for a vinaigrette is typically three parts oil to one part vinegar or lemon juice.

Celery Seed Dressing

½ cup ketchup
1 cup sugar
½ cup apple cider vinegar
⅔ cup vegetable oil
1 tablespoon finely grated onion
1½ teaspoons celery seeds
2 tablespoons paprika
½ teaspoon salt

Whisk all ingredients well (or shake in a jar). Store in refrigerator. Makes 1¾ cups.

Poppyseed Vinaigrette

So good on fresh fruit, Jell-o, or leaf salad.

½ cup sugar
1 teaspoon dry mustard
1 teaspoon salt
¼ teaspoon cracked pepper
¼ cup apple cider vinegar
¾ cup oil
1 tablespoon poppyseed

Blend all dry ingredients and onion in blender; add vinegar. With blender running, add oil in a slow steady stream till well blended. Blend in poppyseed. Makes 1 cup.

Avocado-Mayo Dressing

2 medium avocados, peeled, pitted, sliced
½ cup mayonnaise
I garlic clove, minced
I tablespoon fresh lemon juice
½ teaspoon Greek seasoning

Process all ingredients until creamy. Will keep a day or two in refrigerator in airtight container. Makes 1½ cups.

Editor's Extra: Try this on burgers, too.

Kangaroo Ranch Dressing

This is like outback's . . . delicious!

I teaspoon dry ranch salad dressing mix
I cup mayonnaise
½ cup buttermilk
⅛ teaspoon paprika
⅛ teaspoon garlic powder
¼ teaspoon coarsely ground black pepper

Whisk all ingredients well. Cover bowl and chill dressing at least 30 minutes before serving. Makes 1½ cups.

Creamy Green Yogurt Dressing

½ cup lemon yogurt
¾ cup mayonnaise
I ½ tablespoons rice wine vinegar
½ cup firmly packed fresh parsley
½ cup firmly packed fresh basil
I teaspoon lemon zest
¼ teaspoon salt

Blend all until smooth. Store in a tightly covered container in refrigerator. Makes 1½ cups.

Know where ranch dressing originated, dude? At Hidden Valley Guest Ranch! Steve Henson devised a dry mix to be blended with mayonnaise and buttermilk. He and his wife Gayle served it at their California dude ranch in the late 50's and early 60's. Guests loved it so much they poured it on steaks and ice cream! A customer wanted 300 jars to take back to Hawaii, so Henson offered to provide him with the dried mixture instead. A lucrative business followed. Says Henson: "I gave it away for ten years before I knew I could sell it." The family eventually sold the business.

137

salad dressings were made at home from scratch until restaurant owners began selling their dressings. one of the first was Joe Marzetti, whose restaurant was in columbus, ohio. In 1919, he began bottling a variety of dressings from old country recipes. Kraft entered the industry with its French dressing in 1925. Now over 60 million gallons of a variety of salad dressings are sold in the united states each year, the most popular being ranch.

Blue Cheese or Roquefort Dressing

2 cups mayonnaise
2 tablespoons lemon juice
2 tablespoons grated onion
¼ cup sour cream
1 tablespoon parsley flakes
1 teaspoon minced garlic
½ pound blue cheese or Roquefort, crumbled
Salt and freshly ground black pepper to taste

Mix all ingredients in a large bowl with a wire whisk. Refrigerate. Makes about 3 cups.

Low-Fat Blue Cheese Dressing

1 cup nonfat plain yogurt
1 cup fat-free cottage cheese
2 tablespoons chopped onion
1 teaspoon minced garlic
2 tablespoons crumbled blue cheese

In food processor or blender, process yogurt, cottage cheese, onion, and garlic until smooth. Stir in blue cheese. Refrigerate. Makes about 2¼ cups.

Editor's Extra: Go middle of the road with low-fat yogurt and cottage cheese for a tad more flavor.

Traditional Green Goddess Dressing

1 cup mayonnaise
2 tablespoons lemon juice
½ cup sour cream
2 tablespoons vinegar
1 teaspoon minced garlic
1 tablespoon anchovy paste
1 tablespoon parsley flakes
1 tablespoon grated onion
Salt and freshly ground black pepper to taste
Few drops Tabasco

In 1923, the executive chef at the Palace Hotel in San Francisco concocted Green Goddess dressing to pay tribute to actor George Arliss and his hit play, The Green Goddess.

Blend mayonnaise, lemon juice, and sour cream in blender. Blend in remaining ingredients. Refrigerate. Makes about 2 cups.

Editor's Extra: Nice to add a ripe avocado in the blender.

Sensation Salad Dressing

No need for a lot of salad vegetables. The dressing is the thing. Sensational—no other word for it.

4 ounces Romano cheese, grated
2 tablespoons grated blue cheese
2 cloves garlic, minced finely
3 tablespoons fresh lemon juice
⅓ cup olive oil
⅔ cup vegetable oil
½ teaspoon salt
¼ teaspoon black pepper

Mix all together in a quart jar. Refrigerate.

Just before serving, stir well. For 4 servings, spoon about 3 tablespoons of mixture over ½ head washed, torn, crisped lettuce with plenty of fresh parsley sprinkled on top. Toss all lightly but thoroughly to coat; do not spoon over salads. Makes about 1½ cups.

we've all heard that oil and water don't mix. But why? Why is it necessary to shake a bottle of salad dressing before adding it to a salad? Because it is a mixture of vegetable oil, which is nonpolar, and vinegar, which is polar. Polar and nonpolar molecules do not mix. It's a chemical thing.

Greek Salad Dressing

Like Panera Bread's—delish!

½ cup red wine vinegar
2 teaspoons minced garlic
2 teaspoons minced shallots
2 teaspoons finely chopped fresh oregano
2 teaspoons fresh snipped basil
1 teaspoon whole-grain mustard
Salt and freshly ground black pepper to taste
1½ cups extra virgin olive oil

Whisk all ingredients except oil in a medium bowl. Slowly pour in olive oil while whisking, until emulsed. (You can do this in a processor or blender.) Makes 2 cups.

Choice Salad Dressing

A choice blend . . . no need to refrigerate.

1 cup oil
½ cup vinegar
¼ cup sugar
1 teaspoon each: dry mustard, paprika, garlic salt, celery salt
1 teaspoon grated onion

Put all ingredients in microwave safe bowl. Microwave on HIGH 3 minutes. Beat while it cools till thick. Jar; shake before serving. Makes about 1¾ cups.

Splendid Honey Mustard Dressing

2 cups mayonnaise
1 tablespoon yellow mustard
1 tablespoon Dijon mustard
½ cup Splenda
1 cup milk

Blend well and refrigerate. Makes 3 cups.

Kum-Back Salad Dressing

1 (12-ounce) bottle chili sauce
2 cups mayonnaise
$\frac{1}{4}$ onion, grated
1 teaspoon black pepper
3 teaspoons lemon juice
Dash of Tabasco
1 teaspoon mustard
1 tablespoon Worcestershire
Dash of paprika

Combine all ingredients; mix well; chill. Makes $3\frac{1}{2}$ cups.

Mayo My Way

You simply have to have homemade mayonnaise on those good homegrown tomatoes

—Barbara Moseley

2 egg yolks
1 tablespoon lemon juice or vinegar
$\frac{1}{2}$ teaspoon dry mustard
1 teaspoon salt
Sprinkle of paprika
1–1$\frac{1}{2}$ cups vegetable oil

Beat eggs in cool deep mixing bowl with wire whisk, or electric hand mixer, or in a blender until smooth. Add lemon juice, mustard, salt, and paprika, mixing well. Now is the tricky part. Gradually add oil, drop by drop, until mixture begins to come together. You can add oil a little faster at this point, stopping to scrape down sides of bowl until all is used. Beat until thickened. Refrigerate. Makes $1\frac{1}{4}$–$1\frac{3}{4}$ cups.

Editor's Extra: You may substitute 1 teaspoon Dijon mustard for dry mustard, if desired.

Here's a neat idea: snip open a bag of washed, mixed greens, pour some salad dressing into the bag, and holding the opening closed, gently turn it over and over. Use tongs to place servings onto individual plates.

Russian Tea Room's Russian Dressing

Great on sandwiches or salads, or as a dip.

¾ cup mayonnaise
¼ cup sour cream
⅓ cup chili sauce
½ tablespoon fresh lemon juice
1 tablespoon minced dill pickles
1 tablespoon minced bell pepper (and/or pimentos)
1 tablespoon minced onion
2 teaspoons grated horseradish (or bottled)
1 teaspoon Worcestershire
⅛ teaspoon Tabasco
1 teaspoon sugar
A few grinds black pepper
¼ teaspoon paprika
½ tablespoon minced parsley

Combine all ingredients in a food processor or blender; mix just till blended. Refrigerate. Stir before using. Makes about 1½ cups.

Simple Thousand Island Dressing

⅔ cup mayonnaise
½–⅔ cup chili sauce

Stir together well; refrigerate.

Editor's Extra: You can enhance this with a tablespoon of any or all of the following: pimento, finely chopped green pepper, finely chopped celery, heavy cream. Makes 1¼–1⅓ cups.

Sandwiches

Tea and Brunch Sandwiches

Cold Sandwiches

Hot Sandwiches

Subs and Po-Boys

Wraps and Pockets

Burgers and Dogs

Tea and Brunch Sandwiches

Cucumber Tea Sandwiches

cool, refreshing . . . the first to go.

3 cups diced, seeded, peeled cucumbers, drained
¼ cup diced onion
½ (8-ounce) package cream cheese, softened
¼ cup mayonnaise
3 tablespoons dry Italian dressing mix
⅛ teaspoon Tabasco
Bread rounds

Mix all together, except bread. Spread on bread rounds.

Editor's Extra: Mini seedless cucumbers are perfect for this recipe, as you don't have to peel or seed them.

Sea & Cuke Croissants

8 ounces fresh cooked shrimp, chopped
¾ cup diced crabmeat (may use imitation)
1 cup chopped seeded cucumber
½ cup ranch salad dressing
4 croissants, split
4 leaves Boston lettuce

Mix shrimp, crabmeat, cucumber, and dressing. Line bottom halves of croissants with lettuce; add seafood mixture; cover with top halves. Serves 4.

Editor's Extra: Use mini croissants for elegant finger sandwiches.

To peel or not to peel, that is the question! Lots of vitamins and fiber are usually in that peel, so scrub and rinse, then leave it on. I like to use a vegetable peeler to peel every other strip on cucumbers. Some score down the cuke with the tines of a fork.

144

Craisins Carrot Tea Sandwiches

1 (8-ounce) package cream cheese, softened
1 cup grated carrots
¾ cup shredded sharp Cheddar cheese
⅓ cup chopped toasted pecans
¼ cup craisins
1 loaf raisin bread, crusted

Blend cream cheese in mixer; stir in carrots, Cheddar cheese, pecans, and craisins. Cover and chill until ready to make sandwiches. Spread carrot mixture on bread slices. Good open or closed. Cut into fingers, triangles, or shapes. Makes about 36 sandwiches. *(See full-color photograph in third insert following page 192.)*

Tupper's Favorite Pimento Cheese Sandwiches

Using freshly grated cheese is the secret.

1 (8-ounce) block extra sharp Cheddar cheese
1–2 tablespoons mayonnaise
1 (2-ounce) jar pimento, drained
2 tablespoons cream cheese, softened
2 tablespoons grated onion
1–2 teaspoons Worcestershire
Salt and pepper to taste

Grate cheese in bowl; add enough mayonnaise to make it creamy. Add remaining ingredients and mix well. Spread on your favorite bread for a sandwich, or on crackers for a snack. Keeps well in refrigerator for several days. Makes 3–4 whole sandwiches.

These savory tea sandwiches are reminiscent of British charm, where tea parties and afternoon tea sandwiches originated. You must always remember to cut tea sandwiches into fourths—squares or triangles. or use decorative breads or cut-out shapes.

A tea sandwich should typically be two bites.

Peanut butter & jelly is a classic kids' sandwich, but adults have been known to like them, too. Try some variations on the classic:

- Instead of white bread, try wheat or raisin bread.
- Use crunchy peanut butter
- Try different flavors jelly, jam, or preserves.
- Mix peanut butter with marshmallow crème, caramel, chocolate, butterscotch, or strawberry topping.
- Add raisins or craisins, sliced bananas, or a few chocolate chips.
- Add anything you have in your pantry or fridge—even pickles!

A Honey of a Strawberry Sandwich

⅓ cup peanut butter
1 tablespoon honey
⅓ cup strawberry-flavored cream cheese
1 cup thinly sliced strawberries
8 slices bread of choice

Combine peanut butter and honey. Stir in cream cheese and spread on 4 slices of bread. Top with strawberries. Cover with remaining bread; cut in half.

Apple Cheese Sandwiches

You may need a knife and fork to get every bite.

2 tablespoons mayonnaise
4 slices wheat bread, toasted
1 small apple, thinly sliced
8 ounces Havarti cheese, thinly sliced
2 tablespoons finely chopped toasted walnuts

Spread mayonnaise on bread. Layer apple and cheese slices evenly onto bread slices. Sprinkle with walnuts. Serves 4.

Peachy Cheese Deckers

CHEESE FILLING:
1 cup shredded sharp Cheddar cheese
¼ cup toasted pecans, chopped
¼ cup mayonnaise
Dash of Tabasco

Mix all ingredients together. Add more mayonnaise, if needed, to make desired spreading consistency.

PEACH FILLING:
2 ounces cream cheese, softened
¼ cup peach or pineapple preserves

Mix cream cheese and preserves until well blended.

12 slices white bread
6 slices wheat bread

Remove crust from bread. Spread 1 tablespoon Cheese Filling on white bread slices. Place a piece of wheat bread on each; spread with 2 teaspoons Peach Filling. Top with 6 remaining white bread slices. Cut each sandwich into 4 triangles. Makes 24 triangles.

Olive Nut Spreadwiches

2 (3-ounce) packages cream cheese, softened
½ cup Hellmann's mayonnaise
2 tablespoons liquid from salad olives
Dash of black pepper
1 tablespoon grated onion
1 cup chopped salad olives
½ cup chopped pecans
French or sourdough bread slices

Mix cream cheese and mayonnaise well. Add olive liquid and black pepper; mix well. Add onion, olives, and pecans; mix well. Spread on bread of choice. Store in refrigerator for up to one week. Serves 4.

Editor's Extra: Add some crisp, crumbled bacon for a taste change.

147

The simple ham sandwich is still the most popular sandwich in the United States., and in second place is the BLT.

Extra Special Egg Salad

This is great for breakfast or brunch.

2 eggs, hard-boiled
2 slices bacon, crisply fried, crumbled
¼ teaspoon Greek seasoning
1 tablespoon mayonnaise (more, if needed)
2 English muffin halves, toasted

Coarsely mash eggs with a fork; add bacon, seasoning, and mayonnaise; mix well. Spread on toasted muffin halves. Sprinkle with parsley flakes, if desired. Serves 2.

Hot Mini Ham & Swiss Buns

4 tablespoons butter
2 tablespoons honey mustard
1 tablespoon poppyseed
1 tablespoon grated onion
1 (20-count) package small dinner rolls
5 slices deli ham
5 slices Swiss cheese

Heat first 4 ingredients in saucepan; stir. Split all rolls horizontally; place on big square of foil; paint all insides with heated sauce. Quarter ham and cheese slices, putting 1 of each on each roll; replace tops. Brush remaining sauce on top. Bake in 300° oven 15 minutes. Makes 20.

Editor's Extra: Also good to wrap in foil and bake 10 minutes at 400° for a steamy, soft mini sandwich.

Open-Face Crab English Muffins

I pound lump crabmeat
I cup mayonnaise
3 green onions, chopped
⅓ head iceberg lettuce, chopped
I teaspoon salt
I teaspoon fresh lemon juice
2 tomatoes, sliced
6 English muffins, toasted, buttered
12 slices mozzarella

Combine crabmeat, mayonnaise, onions, lettuce, salt, and lemon juice together. Place tomato slices on each muffin half on a baking pan; add salad, then top with slices of mozzarella. Bake at 350° for 10–15 minutes till cheese is lightly browned. Makes 12.

It is estimated that Americans eat 300 million sandwiches each day! Wow— that's more than one for every man, woman and child in the country!

Ham & Cheese Bagels

1½ cups shredded Monterey Jack cheese
¾ cup diced deli ham or turkey
½ cup mayonnaise
4 bacon strips, cooked, crumbled
4 bagels, split

Mix first 4 ingredients; spread on bagel halves. Place on ungreased baking sheet. Broil 3–5 minutes 6 inches from heat until bubbly and light brown. Serves 4–6.

Biscuit Sandwiches

3 tablespoons butter, softened
5 grand biscuits, baked, split
3 tablespoons cranberry relish
5 slices ham, chicken, or turkey, cut to fit biscuits

Butter biscuit halves and place on baking pan, buttered side up. Broil till just browned. Spread relish on 5 biscuit halves, meat on top, then cover with remaining 5 biscuit halves. Makes 5.

Bacon and Egg Sandwiches

5 hard-boiled eggs, chopped
4 slices bacon, cooked, crumbled
1 tablespoon sweet pickle relish (optional)
¼ cup mayonnaise
Salt and pepper to taste
Lettuce leaves and tomato slices
8 slices white bread

Mix eggs, bacon, relish, mayo, salt and pepper. Spread on 4 bread slices. Top with lettuce and tomatoes, then remaining bread slices.

Editor's Extra: Use real bacon bits to make it easier. Some people like their bread toasted.

Veggie Wedges

¾ (8-ounce) container soft cream cheese with
   garden vegetables
4 (6-inch) pizza crusts
2 cups fresh baby spinach leaves or leaf lettuce
Tomato slices
½ medium orange and yellow bell pepper, sliced
Cucumber slices
Salad seasoning to taste

Spread soft cream cheese evenly on each pizza crusts. On
2 crusts, layer spinach leaves and vegetable slices; sprinkle
with seasoning. Top with remaining 2 crusts, cream cheese
side down. Cut into wedges. Serves 4.

Veggie & Cheese Muffuletta

1 round loaf Italian bread, sliced horizontally
½ cup red wine vinaigrette
½ cup mayonnaise
2 teaspoons capers
1 ripe avocado, peeled, pitted, sliced
¾ cup green salad olives
1 (2¼-ounce) can sliced ripe black olives, drained
½ pound Jarlsberg cheese, thinly sliced, divided
12 fresh basil leaves
4 Roma tomatoes, sliced
4 thin slices sweet onion, separated

Hollow out bottom half of bread to within ¾ inch of
crust. Process or blend red wine vinaigrette, mayonnaise,
and capers well. Spread mixture evenly on inside of top
and bottom of bread. Layer remaining ingredients in bottom half; cover with top and press halves firmly together.
Wrap tightly in plastic for 30 minutes to 1 hour. Unwrap
and slice into wedges. Serves 6–8.

Muffuletta is a type of Sicilian bread, as well as a sandwich that originated in 1906 at Central Grocery in New Orleans by Salvatore Lupo, a Sicilian immigrant. The muffuletta, with numerous alternate spellings, also has numerous pronunciations: locals say, "Muff-uh-LOT-uh"; the proprietors of Central Grocery pronounce it "Moo-foo-LET-ta."

To avoid soggy sandwiches, it helps to spread a light layer of softened butter or cream cheese on the bread. This keeps the bread from absorbing moisture from the filling. Tuck moist ingredients into the center of the sandwich, within slices of meat or cheese so they're not in direct contact with the bread.

Duke of Windsor Sandwich

In 1958, Helen Corbet created this light, attractive sandwich for the Duke of Windsor's visit to Texas.

2 tablespoons sharp Cheddar cheese spread
2 slices egg bread or whole-wheat bread, toasted
1 (½-inch thick) slice pineapple, grilled
2–3 ounces sliced turkey
2 tablespoons Major Grey chutney

Spread cheese on one slice of toasted bread. Place pineapple, then turkey on this slice. Spread chutney on remaining slice of bread and place on top of turkey. Cut sandwich into 4 pieces and serve. Makes one sandwich.

After Thanksgiving Sandwich

3 tablespoons jellied cranberry sauce
2 tablespoons mayonnaise
1 (3-ounce) package cream cheese, softened
4 slices rye bread
2 thick slices turkey breast
Iceberg lettuce leaves, rinsed, dried

Mix cranberry sauce, mayonnaise, and cream cheese; spread on bread slices. Place sliced turkey breast on 2 bread slices. Top with iceberg lettuce leaves. Put remaining bread slices on top; slice diagonally. Serves 2.

Editor's Extra: Can be made into double-decker sandwiches, quartered, and secured with toothpicks.

Open-Face Shrimp Sandwiches

Good on any kind of bread ... or lettuce as a salad.

1 (8-ounce) package cream cheese, softened
⅓ cup mayonnaise
½ pound cooked shrimp, finely chopped
2 tablespoons lemon juice
1 teaspoon chopped parsley
½ teaspoon dried dill
1 baguette, thinly sliced into rounds

Cream together cream cheese and mayonnaise; stir in shrimp, lemon juice, parsley, and dill. Cover and refrigerate a few hours.

Spread shrimp mixture on baguette slices. Cover and refrigerate until ready to serve. Makes 25–30. Serve on tray or platter with lemon slices and parsley.

Lobster Salad Roll

Bring on the fries or chips and sliced dills.

2 cups coarsely chopped cooked lobster
⅔ cup diced celery
¼ cup mayonnaise, or to taste
2 teaspoons finely diced onion
1 teaspoon Old Bay Seasoning
4–5 split toasted hoagie rolls (New England-style, if available)

Have the seafood department in your supermarket steam 2 lobsters. Remove meat; chop and chill. Combine all ingredients. Arrange in buns. Makes 4–5 lobster rolls.

Editor's Extra: You can make this stretch with 2 finely chopped boiled eggs.

153

The legend of the word sandwich says that it was originated in London late one night in 1762 when an English nobleman, John Montagu, the Fourth Earl of Sandwich (1718-1792), was too busy gambling to stop for a meal, so he ordered a waiter to bring him roast-beef between two slices of bread. This apparently kept the Earl from getting his fingers greasy, and therefore he could continue his gambling while eating his snack.

Open-Face Salmon on Rye

1 (8-ounce) package cream cheese, softened
1 teaspoon grated lemon peel
½ teaspoon dried dill weed (or 1 tablespoon fresh)
4 slices rye or wheat bread
16 slices cucumber
½ pound thinly sliced smoked salmon

Combine cream cheese, lemon peel, and dill; mix well. Spread on bread slices. Layer open-face with cucumber slices and salmon. Garnish with fresh dill, if desired. Serves 4.

Chicken Salad Sandwiches

A new "juicy" taste to an old favorite.

1 small apple, peeled, shredded
2 green onions, sliced
½ cup chopped celery
½ teaspoon curry powder
1 ½ cups chopped cooked chicken
¼ cup sour cream
¼ cup mayonnaise
8 slices wheat or white or raisin bread

Mix all ingredients except bread. Spread on 4 slices of bread; top with remaining bread slices. Serves 4.

Traditional Club Sandwich

3 slices bread, toasted
3 tablespoons mayonnaise or honey mustard
3 slices turkey, ham, or roast beef
1 slice Cheddar or Swiss cheese (optional)
2 slices bacon, crisp-cooked
2 leaves lettuce
2–3 slices tomato
Salt and pepper to taste

Spread mayonnaise on 2 slices of toast; add turkey and cheese to one and cover with other, mayo side down. Spread mayo on this top slice, then add remaining ingredients. Add third mayo-ed toast slice and press slightly. Cut into triangles and adhere with cocktail picks. Makes 1 sandwich.

A club sandwich, also called a clubhouse sandwich, has two layers of fillings between three slices of bread. It is often cut into quarters and held together by toothpicks or cocktail sticks. It is thought that the club sandwich was invented in an exclusive Saratoga Springs, New York, gambling club in the late 19th century by a maverick line cook named Danny Mears. This sandwich has appeared on US restaurant menus since 1899, if not earlier.

The Dagwood sandwich has more layers than a club. It was named for a Blondie comic strip character named Dagwood who often raided the refrigerator at night to make a huge sandwich out of anything he could find.

Mama Jean's (Barbara's mother) three-year-old great-granddaughter was visiting and asked for a "samich." Mama Jean asked what she wanted on it, peanut butter and jelly, cheese, etc. The reply was, "No, just a 'samich.'" So she was asked again what she wanted on it. She took a piece of bread and folded it over and said, "That's a samich."

West Coast Focaccia Wedges

1 (14-ounce) can artichoke hearts, drained, chopped
1 red bell pepper, chopped
½ medium cucumber, peeled, chopped
⅓ cup Italian salad dressing
2 focaccia rounds (10–12 inches in diameter)
1 pound sliced smoked turkey, divided
4 slices provolone cheese
1 cup fresh alfalfa sprouts

Mix artichoke hearts, bell pepper, cucumber, and salad dressing. Heat focaccia as directed on package. Place 1 focaccia, flat side up, on cutting board. Layer with half the turkey, all the vegetable mixture, remaining turkey, cheese, and sprouts. Top with remaining focaccia, flat side down. Secure with toothpicks, if necessary. Cut into wedges. Serves 4–8. *(See full-color photograph in third insert following page 192.)*

Naka's Lettuce Sandwich

When Naka Pillman from South Africa stayed with us, she asked me to buy a head of iceberg lettuce and a loaf of white bread. Here's what she did with it!

¼ head iceberg lettuce
2 slices bread
1–2 tablespoons mayonnaise
Salt and lots of black pepper

Naka sliced a couple of generous ¾-inch slices of lettuce, keeping it somewhat intact. She lathered the mayo on both insides of the bread, put the lettuce slices on it, salt and peppered it generously, and bit into it happily. Makes 1 sandwich.

Editor's Extra: I chose to add tomato slices to mine.
—Gwen

Winning Grilled Cheese

Sliced block cheese makes this a real treat.

½ stick butter, softened, divided
8 slices white-wheat bread
I (I-pound) block sharp Cheddar cheese, sliced
Black pepper to taste

Spread half the butter on 8 slices of bread. Place 3 or 4 cheese slices on 4 bread slices and sprinkle with black pepper. Top with remaining bread slices, buttered side down. Coat griddle with ½ remaining butter. Place sandwiches on griddle on medium-high heat. Use sandwich press, if available; otherwise, press sandwiches down with spatula. Toast till cheese is melted and bread is lightly browned. Remove and coat griddle with remaining butter. Turn sandwiches over onto griddle and press down. Toast until lightly browned. Makes 4.

A grilled cheese sandwich and a cup of tomato soup is said to be the #1 choice combo of soup and sandwich.

Kicky Grilled Cheese Sandwich

This grilled cheese has a kick!

2 tablespoons butter
4 slices white or wheat bread
2 slices American cheese
I Roma tomato, thinly sliced
I tablespoon chopped onion
I–2 tablespoons seeded, chopped, jalapeño
   pepper

Heat a griddle or large skillet over medium heat. Spread butter on one side of two slices of bread. Place bread buttered side down on griddle. Put cheese on bread, and top with tomato slices, onion, and jalapeño. Butter one side of remaining bread, and sandwich, buttered side up. Grill on bottom, flip, and grill till brown on other side. Makes 2.

Incorporated in 1639, Sandwich, Massachusetts, is the name of the oldest town on Cape Cod and one of the oldest towns in the United States. It was settled by European immigrants nearly 150 years before the American Revolution.

Hot Chic 'n Cheese Packets

Takes a tad more time, but prepare for taste encores on this one.

4 Italian bread buns (or ciabatta rolls)
3 tablespoons olive oil, divided
3 tablespoons brown mustard
8 ounces Gouda cheese, shredded
½ pound sliced fresh mushrooms
3 green onions, chopped
2 teaspoons minced garlic
2 cups shredded cooked chicken
3 cups baby spinach
Italian seasoning to taste

Make a well in buns by pulling out some of the insides. Drizzle with a tablespoon of olive oil and all the mustard. Sprinkle half the cheese on bottom half of roll. In skillet over medium heat, sauté mushrooms, onions, and garlic in a tablespoon of olive oil; set aside. Put shredded chicken in buns. Add remaining tablespoon of oil to skillet; sauté spinach 2 minutes; season to taste. Divide mushroom mixture and spinach into bun bottoms. Top with remaining cheese; cover with bun tops. Wrap each bun tightly in foil. Bake until cheese melts at 400°, about 20 minutes. Makes 4.

Hot Cheese Sandwich in a Packet

3 cups shredded Swiss cheese
⅔ cup chopped tomato
½ cup chopped green onions
⅔ cup mayonnaise
½ teaspoon Greek seasoning
1 loaf pumpernickel or rye bread

Mix cheese, tomato, green onions, mayonnaise, and seasoning. Spread on bread to make sandwiches, and wrap individually in foil. Bake at 350° for 25 minutes. Serve hot. Makes about 8 sandwiches.

Chicken Canoes

1 (8-ounce) package cream cheese, softened
2 cups cubed cooked chicken
1½ cups shredded Cheddar cheese
1 (4-ounce) can chopped green chiles
3 tablespoons chopped green onions
1½ teaspoons taco seasoning
4 hard rolls

Beat cream cheese until fluffy; add remaining ingredients except bread. Cut top off rolls; carefully hollow out bottoms, leaving ¼-inch shells; discard inside bread. Fill "canoes" with chicken mixture; replace tops, if desired.

On a cookie sheet, bake at 375° for 5–7 minutes or until golden brown. Sprinkle with cilantro, if desired. Serves 4.

Thanks to English chef James Parkinson, the von Essen Platinum club sandwich at the Cliveden House Hotel near London is the world's most expensive sandwich at $197. Weighing just over a pound, the sandwich is made of the likes of Iberico ham, cured for 30 months, quail eggs, white truffles, semi-dried Italian tomatoes, and 24-hour fermented sourdough bread.

Busy Mom's Hobo to Go

Hit the road with one of these cheesy chicken hobos in hand.

½ (8-ounce) package of cream cheese, softened
2 cups cubed cooked chicken
1 cup shredded Colby/Monterey Jack cheese
1 (2-ounce) jar diced pimentos, drained
3 green onions, chopped
½ teaspoon taco seasoning
4–6 sourdough rolls, split

Preheat oven to 375°. Beat cream cheese until fluffy. Stir in chicken, cheese, pimentos, green onions, and seasonings. Pile mixture on bottom half of 4–6 rolls to desired thickness, and top with other half. Place each sandwich in a square of tin foil and fold to make a tight packet. Place packets on a cookie sheet and bake 15 minutes. Makes 4–6.

Editor's Extra: If you prefer a softer bun, use hamburger buns or onion rolls.

160

Buffalo Chicken on a Roll

A really nice combination of flavors.

1 rotisserie chicken, boned, skinned, shredded
½ cup chicken wing hot sauce
¼ cup water
¼ cup mayonnaise
¼ cup ranch dressing
1 cup diced celery
¼ cup crumbled blue cheese
12 Kaiser rolls
2 cups shredded cheese blend

Combine chicken, hot sauce, and water in saucepan; cook 5 minutes, stirring occasionally.

Stir together mayo, dressing, celery, and blue cheese in bowl. Split rolls; toast slightly, if desired. Spoon chicken mixture on bottom, then shredded cheese, then mayo mixture. Close with bun top. Makes 12.

Mesquite Grilled Chicken on a Bun

Nice to serve with cut melon slices, chips, and salad.

4 boneless, skinless chicken breast halves
⅓ cup mesquite-flavored barbecue sauce
4 onion buns, split, toasted
½ teaspoon taco seasoning
¼ cup mayonnaise
1 avocado, peeled, pitted, sliced

Pound chicken between sheets of wax paper to ½-inch thickness. Brush with BBQ sauce. Grill 4–6 inches from medium heat. Cook 10–15 minutes till chicken juices run clear. Stir seasoning into mayo and spread on buns. Place chicken breast half and 2 avocado slices in each bun. Serves 4.

Editor's Extra: If you don't have a meat mallet, use a regular hammer gently, or the edge of a saucer.

The Monte Cristo sandwich is traditionally dipped in its entirety in batter and deep fried. In some regions of the United States it is served grilled, and sometimes open-faced. It can also be served using French toast as a base, with the ham, turkey and cheese piled high and then heated slightly under a broiler. Serve with fruit preserves, powdered sugar, maple syrup, or sweet mustard sauce.

Monte Cristo Sandwiches

Honey mustard
8 slices firm white or rye bread
4 thin slices ham
4 thin slices turkey
4 thin slices Swiss or American cheese
I large egg, slightly beaten
⅓ cup milk
Salt and pepper to taste
2 tablespoons butter

Spread mustard on each slice of bread. Make 4 sandwiches with I slice of ham, turkey, and cheese on each. Combine egg, milk, salt and pepper in a flat bowl. Melt butter in a skillet over low heat. Dip sandwiches quickly in milk-egg mixture, turning to coat each side. Brown both sides in skillet. Serve with chips and pickles. Serves 4.

Avo-Cosmic Sandwich

It's out of this world!

3 tablespoons butter, softened
¼ teaspoon garlic powder
¼ teaspoon dried parsley
2 slices sourdough bread
¼ cup Thousand Island dressing
½ avocado, peeled, pitted, mashed
3 thin slices lean roast beef or turkey breast, warmed (or crisp bacon strips)
3 tablespoons grated Jack or Cheddar cheese

Heat flat griddle. Mix butter, garlic powder, and parsley; spread on outside pieces of bread. Spread dressing on inside of one slice and avocado on the other. Place roast beef on avocado side and top with cheese. Place dressing side of bread on top of meat, and grill on both sides until cheese melts and bread browns. Serves I.

Editor's Extra: Can use French, Italian, baguettes, or any kind of good crusty bakery bread.

Terrific Toasted Tuna Melts

1 (6-ounce) can tuna in water, drained
⅓ cup mayonnaise
¼ cup chopped onion
¼ cup chopped green bell pepper
½ teaspoon dried basil
½ teaspoon dried oregano leaves
8 slices bread
4 slices cheese
2 tablespoons butter, softened

Combine tuna, mayonnaise, onion, green pepper, and seasonings. On 4 bread slices, place cheese slice, tuna mixture, and second bread slice. Spread butter on outside of sandwiches. Brown on both sides in skillet on medium-high. Serves 4.

Mini Crab Melts

1½ cups fresh lump crabmeat
2 hard-boiled eggs, chopped
1 tablespoon lemon juice
⅓ cup mayonnaise
⅓ cup chili sauce
4 mini hamburger buns
2 Cheddar or Swiss cheese slices, cut to fit
Chopped parsley for garnish

Combine crabmeat with remaining ingredients except Cheddar cheese. Spread on split hamburger buns; place on broiler pan. Broil 5 inches from heat 6–7 minutes. Cover with cheese slices and return to oven until cheese is melted. Top with chopped parsley and serve while hot.
(See full-color photograph in third insert following page 192.)

Introduced on July 5, 1937, the name "spam" was chosen from multiple entries in a naming contest to rename Hormel Spiced Ham. In Hawaii, spam is so popular it is sometimes dubbed "The Hawaiian Steak."

Capt'n's Choice Fish Sandwich

Delicious.

4 frozen breaded catfish (or flounder or tilapia) fillets
I tablespoon oil
4 sesame seed buns, split
Tartar sauce
Lettuce, tomatoes, dill pickles

Lightly fry fish fillets in oil until golden brown and flaky inside. Toast split buns lightly and spread tartar sauce on one side. Place fish fillet on tartar sauce and top with lettuce, tomatoes, pickles, and bun top.

Editor's Extra: May put a spoonful of ready-made coleslaw on top of fish fillet instead of lettuce, tomatoes, and pickles.

Hawaiian Spam Bunwiches

12 Hawaiian bread rolls, split
½ cup tartar sauce
2 cups chopped lettuce
3 hard-cooked eggs, sliced
24 dill pickle slices
I (12-ounce) can Spam, sliced to fit rolls
6 slices Swiss cheese
Butter, softened

Spread insides of rolls with tartar sauce. On each half, layer chopped lettuce, egg slices, 2 pickle slices, Spam slices, and cheese slices. Replace tops and butter lightly. Grill or broil a few minutes until golden brown.

Turkey Reubens

A toasty warm sandwich full of Reuben taste.

1 (8-ounce) package smoked turkey
1 (8-ounce) can sauerkraut, drained, rinsed, snipped
2 slices Swiss cheese, halved
8 slices marble rye bread
⅓ cup Thousand Island dressing, divided
¼ cup butter, softened

Layer turkey, sauerkraut, and Swiss cheese on 4 slices of bread that have been spread with salad dressing. Top each with remaining bread slices that have been spread with more salad dressing. Spread outside of each sandwich with butter. Grill sandwiches in heated skillet 4 minutes, turning after 2 minutes. Serves 4.

Open-Faced Reubens

Serve this big baby with a knife and fork—you don't want to leave a morsel.

½ onion, sliced
1 tablespoon butter
¾ pound ground chuck
¼ teaspoon each: salt and pepper
4 slices rye bread
8 ounces sauerkraut, drained, rinsed
4 slices Swiss cheese
Russian dressing
Kosher dill pickle slices

Sauté onion in butter; set aside. Season meat and shape into 4 flat square-ish patties; fry or broil on both sides. Place patties on bread slices; top with sauerkraut, onion, and cheese. Broil on rack in broiler pan until cheese is melted. Serve with dressing and pickle slices. Makes 4.

Russian dressing is actually American, invented in the United States in the late 1800's or early 1900's. Some say it used to include caviar, a food associated with Russia. During the Cold War, many U.S. restaurants referred to it as "Sweet Tomato Dressing" to show their preference to capitalism over communism. Very similar to Thousand Island Dressing, either is often the principal condiment used on Reuben sandwiches.

Corned Beef and Cabbage Sandwiches

Unbelievable flavor!

1 ½ cups finely shredded cabbage
6 tablespoons butter, softened
3 tablespoons honey mustard
12 large slices rye bread
10 ounces corned beef, thinly sliced
3 tablespoons mayonnaise
1 tablespoon horseradish
6 ounces Swiss cheese, thinly sliced

Boil cabbage in lightly salted water 2 minutes only; drain in colander. Mix butter and mustard; spread on one side of bread slices. Divide corned beef on each slice. Mix mayonnaise, horseradish, and cabbage, and spoon onto corned beef. Top with cheese slices, then remaining bread. If desired, grill on griddle with press, turning once. Makes 6 sandwiches.

Macho Meatloaf Sandwich

2 slices sourdough bread or white bread
2 teaspoons each: spicy mustard, ketchup, and/or
   mayonnaise, or to taste
1 slice meatloaf, cut ⅓ inch thick (your favorite
   recipe)
2 teaspoons olive oil, divided
1 slice Monterey Jack cheese
2 slices tomato (optional)

Spread bread with condiments of choice. Brown meatloaf slice on both sides in 1 teaspoon olive oil in skillet. Put browned meatloaf slice on one slice of bread. Add cheese and tomato, if desired. Cover with remaining slice of bread. Heat remaining 1 teaspoon olive oil in skillet or on griddle. Grill over medium heat on both sides, until golden. Makes 1 sandwich.

Cuban Sandwich

1 loaf Cuban bread, hard crust (or French bread)
Mustard
9 thin slices ham
9 thin slices roast pork, hot or cold
9 thin slices Swiss or provolone cheese
9–12 pickle slices

Slice bread open-face so both halves are still barely connected; spread mustard on both halves. Layer with ham and then roasted pork. Add cheese and a few pickle slices. Spray sandwich press with a little butter-flavored Pam, or brush softened butter on outside of bread. Place sandwich in sandwich press and press down until cheese is melted and bread is slightly hard to the touch. Slice diagonally into 3 or 4 sandwiches.

Editor's Extra: No press? Place sandwich in a hot skillet and press down on it with a heavy kitchen object, maybe a baking pan (some, believe it or not, use a brick wrapped in foil).

Cuban bread has a crack or "bloom" on the top of its crust, which happens naturally during baking. Italian or French breads are good substitutes, but Cubans say it's not a real Cuban sandwich without Cuban bread.

Philly Cheesesteak Sandwich

½ pound rib eye, partially frozen
1 medium onion, sliced thinly
½ green pepper, sliced thinly
2 tablespoons vegetable oil
Salt and coarsely ground black pepper
4 provolone cheese slices or ½ cup Cheese Whiz, melted
2 Kaiser or hoagie rolls
Pickled peppers or dill pickle spears

Slice cold meat thinly. Sauté onion and pepper slices in oil in cast iron skillet or on grill top; add steak slices and cook until meat lightly browns; add salt and pepper to taste. Heap cooked mixture on two sides of pan; divide cheese over meat until melted.

Slice rolls lengthwise. Using a spatula, scoop each mixture and lay on bread bottoms with cheese on top. Cover, slice, and serve with pickles. Makes 2 sandwiches.

In 1930, a hot dog vendor in South Philadelphia, Pat Olivieri, put some beef and onions on his grill. A taxi driver smelled it cooking and asked to buy one. Rumor spread, and cabbies came from all over to get them. Pat's King of Steaks added cheese, or maybe it was Geno's across the street . . . they are friendly rivals to this day.

Why is the diagonal slice so popular? Perhaps because it makes each half of the sandwich look bigger. And for sure the first bite is more inviting. Well, anyway, what sandwich wants to be a square when it could have a sharper point?

Stromboli-o-li Bread

A yummy hot giant "sandwich" just waiting to be sliced.

⅓ pound bulk Italian sausage
⅓ pound ground beef
¾ cup frozen seasoning blend (chopped onion, celery, pepper)
½ cup sliced fresh mushrooms
⅓ cup tomato paste
½ cup water
2 tablespoons grated Parmesan cheese
I teaspoon Italian seasoning
I loaf Italian bread
6 slices mozzarella cheese, divided

Brown meats in large skillet with seasoning blend and mushrooms over medium heat; drain. Stir in tomato paste, water, Parmesan, and seasoning. Simmer 5 minutes till thickened.

Cut off top third of bread loaf; hollow out bottom, leaving ½-inch shell. Insert 3 mozzarella cheese slices on bottom; top with sausage mixture and rest of cheese. Replace bread top; wrap loaf in foil. Bake at 400° for 15–20 minutes until cheese is melted. Let stand a few minutes before slicing. Serves 6–8.

Barbecue Brisket Sandwiches

2 tablespoons Worcestershire
2 teaspoons Cajun seasoning
1 tablespoon brown sugar
1 (4- to 5-pound) brisket
1 cup barbecue sauce
2 tablespoons mustard
French bread or hamburger buns

Mix Worcestershire, seasoning, and brown sugar; rub into all sides of brisket. Bake in heavy pan covered tightly with foil at 225° for 8 hours or overnight.

Remove brisket to plate. Pour off all but $\frac{1}{4}$ cup liquid. Stir in barbecue sauce and mustard. Slice brisket thin and return to pan. Bake 45 minutes at 325°. Serve on sliced French bread or toasted buns. Serves 8–12.

Meats are easier to slice when cold. So if you need thin slices for sandwiches, be sure your cooked roast has been refrigerated for awhile.

Two-For-One Rib-Eye Sandwiches

An excellent way to stretch one rib-eye to make two sandwiches. Now I do this on purpose!

1 (4- to 5-ounce) rib-eye
3 tablespoons butter, divided
$\frac{1}{2}$ teaspoon oil
$\frac{1}{2}$ onion, halved, sliced
1 tablespoon soy sauce
2 hamburger buns or small hoagie buns

Preheat oven to 450°. Heat cast-iron skillet; brown rib-eye in 1 tablespoon butter and oil on medium-high heat for 2 minutes. DO NOT TURN. Put skillet in oven for 8–11 minutes till desired doneness.

Meanwhile sauté onion in small skillet in remaining 2 tablespoons butter. Stir in soy sauce. Toast buns and drizzle some of the meat juices on each inside. Slice rib-eye thinly and divide on buns; top with sautéed onions.

Sandwiches are not the easiest things to freeze for later, but it can be done.

Spread soft butter on inside slices of bread; this keeps the bread from getting soggy. Add meat and cheese; close and wrap in tin foil. Make several at one time and freeze in zipper bag(s) for up to a week.

You can freeze jelly and honey on buttered or peanut buttered sandwiches.

Don't freeze vegetables or fruits or mayonnaise on sandwiches. Small amounts of condiments such as ketchup, mustard, or relish should do just fine.

Steak 'n Mushroom Rolls

1 pound thinly sliced grilled or broiled steak
1 large portobello mushroom, sliced, sautéed, or grilled
½ red bell pepper, cut into thin strips
1 tomato, thinly sliced
¼ cup balsamic vinaigrette
Lettuce leaves
4–6 rolls, tortilla wraps, or pita pockets

Marinate first 4 ingredients in balsamic vinaigrette; refrigerate 2 hours or more. Put lettuce leaves on warmed or toasted bread on plate and top with steak mixture. Serves 4–6.

Easy Pepperoni Calzones

1 (13.8-ounce) tube refrigerated pizza crust
1 cup shredded mozzarella cheese
32 slices pepperoni
¾ cup ricotta or cottage cheese
¾ cup chopped sweet bell pepper
¼ cup finely chopped onion

Roll pizza crust into a 12-inch square. Cut into 4 squares. Over half of each, sprinkle 2 tablespoons mozzarella cheese, 8 slices pepperoni, and 3 tablespoons ricotta. Divide pepper and onion onto each square; top with remaining 2 tablespoons ricotta. Fold plain dough over filling, pressing edges with a fork to seal. Place on lightly greased baking sheet. Bake 13–18 minutes at 400° till golden brown. Serves 4.

Griddle Pizza Sandwiches

¼ cup butter, softened
6 slices wheat bread
1 (15-ounce) can chili, warmed
½ teaspoon Italian seasoning
¾ cup pizza sauce
1–1½ cups shredded part-skim mozzarella cheese

Butter bread on both sides. Toast bread on a greased griddle until lightly browned on one side. Turn; quickly spoon ¼ cup chili on each slice. Sprinkle with Italian seasoning. Top each with 2 tablespoons pizza sauce and 3 tablespoons cheese. Cook until bottom turns golden brown and cheese melts. Serves 4–6.

Pizza in a Crescent

½ cup chopped bell pepper
⅓ cup chopped onion
1 pound bulk pork sausage, crumbled
1 (15-ounce) can pizza sauce, divided
2 (8-ounce) cans refrigerated crescent rolls
4 slices mozzarella cheese, halved

In large skillet, cook pepper, onion, and sausage until sausage is no longer pink; drain. Stir in 3 tablespoons pizza sauce. Separate dough into 8 rectangles, pressing middle perforations to seal. Place ¼ cup sausage mixture and a folded cheese slice on one end of each rectangle. Fold dough in half over filling; press edges to seal. Place on ungreased baking pan. Bake at 375° for 15–18 minutes or until golden brown. Heat remaining pizza sauce and serve with crescents. Serves 6–8.

Mighty Caesar Subs

This gets high marks in taste.

4 submarine sandwich rolls
⅓ cup Caesar dressing
1 rotisserie chicken, skinned, thinly sliced
4 slices Swiss or provolone
4 slices tomato
4 lettuce leaves
½ sweet onion, thinly sliced

Cut rolls in half and spread inside with dressing. Layer one side with chicken, cheese, tomato, lettuce, and onion. Press top halves on gently. Cut each in half diagonally. Serves 4.

Everybody Loves Meatball Subs

1 (8-ounce) package frozen Italian meatballs
1 (15-ounce) can pizza sauce
4 hoagie buns, split
1 cup shredded mozzarella cheese

In skillet, cook meatballs over medium heat 5 minutes, turning frequently; add pizza sauce. Heat through. Place 4 meatballs on each hoagie bun bottom. Spoon sauce over and sprinkle with cheese; cover with bun top. Makes 4.

Juicy Pig Hoagies

SOUTHWESTERN SALSA COLESLAW:
I large bag shredded coleslaw mix
¼ cup sour cream
½ cup salsa ranch salad dressing
Coarse-ground pepper to taste

Combine ingredients.

PULLED PORK:
I (3- to 4-pound) pork tenderloin
I tablespoon barbecue rub (your favorite)
6 ounces candied jalapeños or jalapeño pepper jelly
¼ cup chipotle mustard or hot brown mustard
I cup sweet barbecue sauce
8 hoagie buns

Rub roast with seasoning rub and cook in slow cooker on LOW 8 hours. Shred pork with 2 forks, right in the slow cooker. Combine next 3 ingredients and stir into shredded pork. Cover cooker and cook on LOW until pork is thoroughly heated. Serve on hoagies with Southwestern Salsa Coleslaw. Makes 4 hoagies.

Editor's Extra: You may substitute 4–6 chicken breasts for pork tenderloin and continue as directed. Also good on baguettes.

A serrated knife is best for slicing sandwiches, especially if the bread is thick or crusty. Hold the sandwich securely with your other hand without pressing down. A cocktail toothpick with an olive or pickle slice looks attractive while it holds it all together.

173

According to many, the Hoagie originated in an area of Philadelphia, Pennsylvania, known as Hog Island, which was home to a shipyard during World War 1 (1914-1918). Italian immigrants working there would bring giant sandwiches made with cold cuts, spices, oil, lettuce, tomatoes, onions, and peppers for their lunches. The workers were nicknamed "hoggies." Over the years, the name was attached to the sandwiches, but with a different spelling— "hoagies."

Superfast Hoagies

$\frac{1}{4}$ cup honey mustard salad dressing
4 hoagie buns, split
4 large lettuce leaves
$\frac{3}{4}$ pound deli sliced meats (salami, turkey, beef, ham)
I large tomato, sliced thinly
4 Pepper Jack or Colby Jack cheese slices

Spread salad dressing on inside of buns. Layer one side with lettuce leaf, meats folded in half, tomato slices, and cheese slices, halved. Cover with bun tops and slice diagonally. Serves 4.

Pizza Hoagies

I pound lean ground beef
$\frac{3}{4}$ cup frozen seasoning blend (chopped onion, celery, pepper)
$\frac{3}{4}$ cup pizza sauce
$\frac{1}{4}$ cup ketchup
3 tablespoons brown sugar
4 hoagie buns
I cup shredded mozzarella cheese

Brown ground beef; drain; add seasoning blend. Add pizza sauce, ketchup, and brown sugar. Spoon onto buns and scatter cheese on top. Slice diagonally. Serves 4.

Open-Face Roast Beef and Gravy Po-Boats

only takes 10 minutes to prep. sloppy and delicious. serve with a fork and a sharp knife. yum!

1 (5- to 6-pound) beef pot roast
1 teaspoon minced garlic
2 (10¾-ounce) cans cream of mushroom soup
1 (1-ounce) package onion soup mix
1 cup hot water
1 loaf French bread

Put all but bread in crockpot and cook on HIGH 3–4 hours or on LOW 8 hours. Remove roast to platter, cover and chill at least an hour (or overnight) for easier slicing, but good right away. Put split bread sections on plates, top with roast slices, and spoon on the gravy. Serves 10–16.

Dressed Oyster Po-Boys

Oysters (1 per inch of bread)
Corn flour, salt, pepper
Po-boy bread or French mini-loaves
Mayonnaise or tartar sauce
Tomato slices
Shredded lettuce
Dill pickle slices

Dip drained oysters in seasoned corn flour and fry quickly in very hot oil; drain on paper towels. Heat French bread in oven just enough to get hot—do not toast. Split and spread with mayonnaise. Cover with hot oysters, tomatoes, lettuce, and a few pickles. Put top half on and mash it down with your palm; cut in 6-inch slices. Offer ketchup, cocktail sauce, and Tabasco.

Editor's Extra: This works just as well with shrimp, crawfish, catfish, softshell crab . . . whatever you want.

Po-boys are different from subs and gyros because of the bread. Louisiana French bread is different from a baguette in that it is lighter and has a very flaky crust—you can't eat it without making crumbs. The humidity in the Deep South causes the yeast to be more active, so it has a soft, airy center. Typically, it comes in two foot-long "sticks." A po-boy can be the whole thing, or a half, called a "shorty."

175

Po-boys are served hot, and may include fried shrimp, oysters, soft shell crab, catfish, crawfish, sausage, or roast beef and gravy. And always, you are asked, "Ya want cha sandwich dressed?" This would be lettuce, tomato, and mayonnaise; pickles and onion are optional. And mustard goes on the non-seafood po-boys. course-grained creole mustard is referred to as "hot" mustard; the standard yellow is "regular." You can use shredded green cabbage instead of lettuce like the popular Mother's Restaurant on Poydras Street in New Orleans.

Roast Po-Boys in a Packet

Be ready for a burst of roast aromatherapy!

BUTTER-MUSTARD SAUCE:

1 stick butter
2 tablespoons sugar
3 tablespoons mustard
2 tablespoons poppyseed
2 tablespoons grated onion

Melt butter in small pot; stir in remaining ingredients.

PO-BOYS:

1 (1- to 1½-pound) pork tenderloin
½ cup water
1 teaspoon Cajun seasoning
1 long loaf French bread
1 pound Swiss or provolone cheese

Cook pork tenderloin in pressure cooker for 12 minutes at 7.5 pounds pressure with water and seasoning.

Preheat oven to 325°. Split bread loaf horizontally; paint both halves with Butter-Mustard Sauce. Layer cheese slices, then roast slices on top. Cut into desired number of po-boys (4–6). Wrap each section in foil and bake 14 minutes. Keep wrapped till ready to serve. Offer lettuce, sliced tomatoes, and pickles.

Editor's Extra: Roast the pork loin 40–50 minutes at 350°, if desired.

Sweet and Sour Chicken Wraps

1½ cups chopped cooked chicken
1 cup packaged coleslaw mix
¼ cup slivered almonds
⅓ cup sliced water chestnuts
½ red bell pepper, cut into thin strips
4 (8-inch) flour tortillas
½ cup sweet and sour sauce

Mix chicken, coleslaw, almonds, water chestnuts, and pepper strips. Spoon evenly down center of each tortilla. Top evenly with sweet and sour sauce; roll up. Serves 4.

Chicken Caesar Salad Wraps

1 (7½-ounce) package Caesar salad mix
1 cup chopped cooked chicken
4 (8-inch) flour tortillas
2 tablespoons shredded fresh Parmesan cheese

Combine all contents of packaged Caesar salad except croutons with chicken. Spoon mixture onto tortillas. Crush croutons from salad package; sprinkle over salad along with Parmesan. Roll up each tortilla. Serves 4.

Wrap Around the Pepperoni

⅔ cup pizza sauce
4 (8-inch) flour tortillas
1 cup shredded mozzarella cheese
½ (3½-ounce) package pepperoni slices

Spread pizza sauce over tortillas to within 1 inch of edges. Sprinkle with cheese; put pepperoni slices down center. Roll up each tortilla; wrap in foil. Place in 350° oven 10–12 minutes or till cheese is melted. Serves 4.

wraps, or wrap sandwiches, have not been around very long at all, but their popularity has taken off quite rapidly. These sandwiches are variations of traditional sandwiches with different breads. Any type of flat bread is spread with a hot or cold sandwich filling, rolled up, and eaten out of hand. You can use flavored tortillas, cracker bread, rice paper wrappers, cooled crêpes, split pita breads, or sturdy lettuce leaves.

A Mighty Good Mushroom Wrap

12 ounces portobello mushroom caps, cleaned, sliced
1 medium onion, halved, sliced
1 medium red bell pepper, cut in strips
1½ tablespoons oil
1 teaspoon lemon pepper
1 teaspoon salt
4 (8-ounce) flour tortillas (tomato-basil is good)
¼ cup mayonnaise

Cook mushrooms, onion, and bell pepper in oil in large skillet over medium-high heat. Season, stir, and cook 10 minutes till tender. Spread each tortilla with a tablespoon of mayonnaise. Spoon vegetables down center of each tortilla; roll up. Serves 4.

Hotty Toddy Ham Wraps

4 (8-inch) flour tortillas
¼ cup Cheddar cheese spread
1½ cups diced cooked ham
2 tablespoons mayonnaise
1 teaspoon prepared mustard
1 tablespoon sweet pickle relish
1 cup creamy coleslaw

Spread bottom half of each tortilla with cheese spread. Combine ham, mayonnaise, mustard, and pickle relish; mix well. Divide mixture in strips across tortillas; top with coleslaw. Roll tortillas around filling from bottom edge. About ⅓ way up, fold in edges; continue to roll up. Wrap securely in wax paper. Microwave on HIGH 30 seconds each, or until thoroughly heated. Serves 4.

Baked Ham and Cheese Pizza Pockets

1 cup shredded mozzarella cheese
1 cup chopped cooked ham
$\frac{1}{4}$ cup chopped bell pepper
$\frac{1}{2}$ teaspoon dried basil
1 (10-ounce) can refrigerated pizza crust

Preheat oven to 425°. Mix all ingredients except pizza crust. Place pizza dough on greased cookie sheet. Press out with hands to 8x14-inch rectangle. Cut into 4 separate rectangles. Spoon $\frac{1}{2}$ cup ham mixture onto half of each rectangle; fold dough over filling. Press edges with fork to seal; prick tops with fork. Bake 10–15 minutes till golden brown. Serves 4.

Pocket Full of Nuggets

These are soft, crunchy, drippy, and tasty!

1 egg
$\frac{1}{4}$ cup milk
1 cup bread crumbs
$\frac{1}{4}$ cup grated Parmesan cheese
1 pound boneless, skinless chicken breasts, cut bite-size
$1\frac{1}{3}$ cups shredded lettuce
4 (6-inch) pita breads with pockets, cut in half
$\frac{1}{2}$ cup ranch dressing or barbecue sauce

Beat egg and milk together in one bowl; combine bread crumbs and cheese in another. Dip chicken into egg mixture, then bread crumbs, patting nuggets to help crumbs stick. Bake nuggets on greased baking sheet in 400° oven 8–10 minutes till golden. Divide lettuce between pita pockets. Put 3 or 4 chicken nuggets in each half. Drizzle 2 tablespoons dressing or sauce over each serving. Serves 4.

Editor's Extra: Make this simpler by using packaged frozen breaded chicken nuggets.

Milano Chicken Pitas

A great hot on-the-go dinner.

2 tablespoons olive oil
½ medium onion, sliced
1 cup julienned carrots
1 cup chopped fresh broccoli
1 cup cubed cooked chicken
1 (7-ounce) jar roasted sweet red peppers,
   drained, chopped
¼ cup chicken broth
1 teaspoon Italian seasoning
4 (6-inch) pita breads, halved
½ cup shredded Cheddar cheese
¼ cup shredded mozzarella cheese

In oil in a large skillet, sauté onion, carrots, and broccoli 4–5 minutes till tender. Stir in chicken, red peppers, broth, and seasoning. Bring to a boil; reduce heat; simmer, uncovered 5–6 minutes till heated through. Spoon into pita bread halves; sprinkle with cheeses. Heat in 400° oven or grill a few minutes to warm. Serves 4. *(See full-color photograph in third insert following page 192.)*

Hero Gyros

Along with the slow rotisserie cooking of the lamb or pork or beef, the sauce is the thing! This is the true sauce for gyros.

Thinly sliced roasted lamb, beef, or pork
Pita pockets or flat bread
Tzatziki Sauce

Fill bread with meat, then, if desired, add chopped tomatoes and lettuce; cover with sauce, and wrap or roll in paper to serve.

TZATZIKI SAUCE:
1 medium cucumber, peeled, seeded, chopped
1 pint plain yogurt, drained
$\frac{1}{8}$ teaspoon kosher salt
1 tablespoon finely minced garlic
1 tablespoon olive oil
2 teaspoons red wine vinegar
4 mint leaves, finely minced

Put chopped cucumber in a tea towel, then squeeze out the juice. Combine pulp with remaining ingredients. Makes $1\frac{1}{2}$ cups and should keep for a week in the frig.

Editor's Extra: Drain yogurt in a tea towel suspended over a bowl in the refrigerator for about 2 hours; discard the juice.

Gyros are made from meat which has been placed on a tall vertical spit, which turns in front of a source of heat. The rate of roasting can be adjusted by varying the heat and/or the distance between the heat and the meat. The meat is sliced vertically and is generally served in an oiled, fried piece of pita, rolled up with lettuce, tomatoes, and sauce.

Henry VIII, who ruled England from 1509 until his death in 1547, was known for his voracious appetite. He enjoyed banquets so much that he extended the kitchen of Hampton Court Palace to fill 55 rooms. The 200 members of the kitchen staff provided meals of up to 14 courses for the 600 people in the king's court. He served such exotic dishes as grilled beaver's tails, whale meat, roasted swan and boar's head. Yum?

Quick-To-Fix Burritos

Kids love and can fix these themselves.

I cup grated Cheddar cheese
6 (6-inch) flour tortillas
I (15-ounce) can chili with beans

Divide cheese among tortillas, spreading down middle of each. Spoon chili over cheese. Roll each tortilla, then wrap in a paper towel. Microwave one at a time 25 seconds on HIGH, or more to heat through.

Queso Wraps

I (6-ounce) package fajita-seasoned, fully cooked beef or chicken strips
½ red onion, thinly sliced
I cup shredded Monterey Jack cheese
⅔ cup salsa
I cup white queso cheese dip
3 large flour tortilla wraps
Chopped lettuce, tomatoes, and sour cream for topping

Heat beef or chicken strips (separately, if using both) in microwave-safe dishes for 3 minutes. Microwave queso dip on HIGH 2 minutes, or until melted.

Divide beef or chicken strips in center of each tortilla. Add some onion and cheese. Fold bottom half of tortilla halfway up the mixture in the center. Start rolling one side toward opposite side. Cover bottom half of wrapped tortilla in a square of wax paper to prevent drips. Pour salsa, then melted queso over open end of wrap. Top with lettuce, tomatoes, and sour cream when serving. Serves 3.

Build-Your-Own Tacos

A delicioso Mexican "sandwich."

1 pound ground chuck
1 package dry taco seasoning
Hard taco shells

Brown meat with seasoning per package directions. Place 2–3 tablespoons mixture into each shell. Offer Condiments in separate containers to build your own taco.

CONDIMENTS:
Shredded cheese
Shredded lettuce
Chopped tomatoes
Chopped black olives
Chopped onion
Salsa or picante sauce
Sour cream or guacamole

Editor's Extra: Use 6-inch flour tortillas if you prefer soft tacos.

Black and Blue Sliders

1 pound lean ground beef
¼ cup Italian bread crumbs
¼ cup sour cream
1 tablespoon minced onion
1 egg, beaten
½ teaspoon salt
¼ teaspoon pepper
¾ cup blue cheese crumbles
10 party rolls, split

Mix ground beef, bread crumbs, sour cream, and onion. With hands, mix in beaten egg, salt, and pepper. Shape into 10 small patties.

Place on heated outdoor grill 3 minutes, then cover and cook 4 minutes more, turning once. Add cheese for last 2 minutes.

Indoors, broil on broiler pan 4–6 inches from heat 3 minutes each side. Add cheese for last 3 minutes.

Place on toasted buns with condiments of choice. Makes 10 sliders. *(See full-color photograph in third insert following page 192.)*

Sliders have been around a long time from Krystal and White Castle. Today the word has a new meaning— a little burger. Not so thin as the original sliders, the new trendy ones are fatter and fancier.

Awesome Hamburgers

2 pounds lean ground beef
⅓ cup finely chopped onion
⅓ cup finely chopped green bell pepper
½ cup crushed cornflakes
2 tablespoons Worcestershire
2 tablespoons milk
Salt, pepper, and garlic salt to taste
1 egg
8 hamburger buns

Combine ground beef, onion, bell pepper, cornflakes, Worcestershire, milk, seasonings, and egg. Form into 8 hamburgers; brown in large skillet. Serve on lightly toasted buns with whatever hamburger condiments you desire.

Cheese-Stuffed Burgers

1½ pounds hamburger meat
2 tablespoons dry Italian salad dressing mix
4 slices mozzarella cheese
4 whole-wheat buns
Lettuce, tomatoes, pickles

Mix hamburger with salad dressing mix. Form into 8 thin patties. Cut cheese to fit patties and place onto 4 patties, cover with remaining 4 patties; pinch patty edges to seal around cheese. Grill about 12 minutes. Serve on lightly toasted buns, and add condiments of choice.

The word hamburger first appeared in English in the late 1800's, and is thought to have come from the town of Hamburg, Germany. It was originally called "hamburger steak."

Juicy French Dip Burgers

Talk about taste!

1 (1-ounce) package dry onion soup mix
1¼ cups beef broth (or water), divided
1 pound ground beef
½ teaspoon Cajun seasoning
1 loaf French bread

Dissolve soup mix in ½ cup broth or water. Stir well; add 2 tablespoons of this to ground beef and mix; add seasoning. Add remaining ¾ cup water or broth to soup mix mixture; set aside. Shape meat into 4 oval-shaped patties; grill or broil till done, 10–12 minutes. Cut French bread into 8 diagonal slices; grill briefly till toasted. Meanwhile, heat reserved soup mix. Place burgers between 2 slices of bread. Serve with hot broth for dipping.

Mushroom Hamburgers

2 pounds ground chuck
2 tablespoons Worcestershire
12 saltine crackers, finely crushed
½ teaspoon black pepper
½–1 pint mushrooms, thinly sliced
½ onion, thinly sliced
½ stick butter
8 hamburger or hoagie buns

Mix first 4 ingredients; form into patties and fry in large skillet till browned on both sides and cooked through. Remove patties and drain. In same skillet, sauté mushrooms and onion in butter till limp. Serve patties on toasted buns with a generous scoop of mushrooms and onion. Makes 8.

Blue Cheese Burgers

The caramelized onions make these super delicious!

1¼ pounds lean ground beef
1 ounce blue cheese, crumbled
½ teaspoon each: salt and pepper
1 Vidalia onion, sliced, separated, sautéed
4 hamburger buns

Mix ground beef, blue cheese, salt and pepper. Shape into patties. Grill patties on preheated grill 4–6 inches from medium heat about 10 minutes, till cooked through, turning once. (Or broil 4–6 inches from heat.) Grill or broil split buns briefly to heat; put patties and onion slices on buns. Serves 4 deliciously.

Supercalifragilistic Cheeseburgers

They are expialidociously delicious!

1½ pounds ground beef
¼ cup milk
¼ cup fine cracker crumbs
1 teaspoon Cajun seasoning
⅓ cup chili sauce
3 tablespoons pickle relish
2 teaspoons mustard
6 onion burger buns, buttered, toasted
6 slices provolone cheese

Form ground beef, milk, crumbs, and seasoning into 6 patties. Combine chili sauce, relish, and mustard; spread on each bun. Pan-fry patties about 12 minutes, turning once; place on buns. Top with cheese. Place under broiler, cooking until cheese begins to melt. Cover with bun top. Makes 6.

Mexican Cheeseburgers

1 pound lean ground beef
½ cup finely sliced green onions
1 teaspoon minced fresh cilantro
2 teaspoons minced garlic
2 teaspoons taco seasoning
1 (7-ounce) can chopped green chiles
6 tablespoons salsa
6 slices Monterey Jack cheese
Shredded lettuce
6 hamburger buns

Combine beef, green onions, cilantro, garlic, and taco seasoning. Shape into 6 patties and broil or grill till cooked through. Heat green chiles, salsa, and cheese together. To serve, place meat patty on shredded lettuce on buns; spoon sauce over meat. Garnish with avocado slices, if desired. Makes 6.

At $99, the Double Truffle Hamburger at DB Bistro Moderne in Manhattan contains three ounces of rib meat mixed with truffles and foie gras stuffed inside seven ounces of sirloin steak and served on a Parmesan and poppyseed bun, with salad and truffle shavings. (For the less extravagant, the single Truffle is only $59.)

But wait! A neighborhood restaurant in New Orleans boasts: World's Most Expensive Hamburger $100— Hamburger $7 comes with really nice wine $93.

"It seems to me that our three basic needs, for food and security and love, are so entwined that we cannot think of one without the other . . . since we're forced to nourish ourselves, why not do it with all possible skill . . . and ever-increasing enjoyment."

—M.F.K. Fisher

Cajun Burgers

1 cup frozen seasoning blend (chopped onion, celery, pepper)
1 tablespoon margarine
½ tablespoon Tabasco
1–2 teaspoons Cajun seasoning
1 pound lean ground beef
4 onion buns, toasted
Mayonnaise, Creole mustard, lettuce, tomatoes, pickles

Sauté seasoning blend in margarine in skillet. Add Tabasco and seasoning to taste. In a bowl, mix this with ground beef; form into 4 patties. Grill or broil till cooked through. Serve on toasted buns with mayo, mustard, lettuce, tomato, and pickle slices.

Editor's Extra: Want a different boost of flavor? Try horseradish mayonnaise with yellow or no mustard.

Pizza Burgers

1 pound ground beef
½ cup seasoned bread crumbs
1 egg
Salt and pepper to taste
2 tablespoons oil
1 (8-ounce) can tomato sauce
½ teaspoon Italian seasoning
6 slices mozzarella
4–6 hamburger buns

Combine ground beef, bread crumbs, egg, salt and pepper; shape into 4–6 burgers. Fry (in a little oil) burgers on both sides till done. Remove burgers and pour off excess fat. Add tomato sauce, a little water to rinse can, and seasoning. Bring to a boil; stir; simmer. Return burgers, cover, and cook 15 minutes. Just before serving, place a slice of mozzarella on each burger, and replace cover just to melt cheese. Serve on buttered, toasted buns. Serves 4–6.

Oriental Hamburgers

1 pound ground beef
1 teaspoon minced garlic
2 green onions, chopped
1 tablespoon soy sauce
Dash of pepper
1 egg
1 teaspoon brown sugar
1 teaspoon grated gingerroot, or $\frac{1}{8}$ teaspoon
  dried ginger
4 sesame hamburger buns

Combine ingredients and shape into patties. Grill, broil (3–5 minutes on each side), or pan fry till done. Serve on buns. Yields 4 servings.

Chili Bean Burgers

Good open-face on half a bun . . . or topped.

2 pounds lean ground beef
1 (4-ounce) can diced green chiles
1½ cups finely shredded Cheddar cheese, divided
1 teaspoon taco seasoning
4 hamburger buns
2 (15-ounce) cans chili with beans, heated
¾ cup chopped red onion

Combine ground beef, green chiles, ¾ cup Cheddar cheese, and seasoning in bowl; mix well. Shape into 8 patties. Grill 4–6 inches over hot coals to desired doneness, turning once or twice. Move patties to edge of grill. Grill buns 1 minute cut-side-down on grill. Arrange patties on buns on serving platter. Top with chili; sprinkle with remaining cheese and onion. Makes 8.

Parmigiana Venison Burgers

1 ¼ pounds ground venison
½ teaspoon garlic salt
¼ cup minced onion
1 (8-ounce) can tomato sauce
1 cup grated mozzarella
1 teaspoon Italian seasoning
6–8 hamburger buns

Preheat oven to 400°. Mix meat, garlic, salt, and onion. Shape into 6–8 patties, and place in greased baking dish. Cover with tomato sauce. Sprinkle with cheese and seasoning. Bake in oven 30 minutes. Serve on toasted buns. Makes 4–6 servings.

No Guilt Turkey Burgers

Excellent with BBQ sauce, lettuce, and tomato slices.

1 pound ground turkey
1 small zucchini, shredded
½ cup crushed cornflakes
1 egg white
2 tablespoons Worcestershire
1 tablespoon parsley
Salt and pepper to taste
1 ½ cups frozen seasoning blend (chopped onion, celery, pepper)*
4 hamburger buns

Combine all ingredients except buns in large bowl; mix well. Form into 4 soft patties. Use spatula to transfer to broiler pan or fine wire vegetable rack for grilling. Cook well. Serve on buns. Serves 4.

*Let frozen veggies thaw a little, then squeeze with paper towels before adding to mixture.

Veggie Cheeseburgers

**4 (3.2-ounce) packages all vegetable protein
   patties**
4 whole-wheat or sourdough buns, toasted
½ cup guacamole
4 slices Monterey Jack cheese
4 big tomato slices
Alfalfa or broccoli sprouts

Cook patties per package directions. Spread guacamole on buns. Place patties on buns, topping with cheese and tomatoes.

Editor's Extra: Chipotle mayonnaise can sub for the guacamole for a different taste.

Biscuit Burgers

I pound lean ground beef
I teaspoon Italian seasoning
I (8-count) can jumbo buttermilk biscuits
Mustard, ketchup, pickle relish
4 thin slices sweet onion

In bowl, mix ground beef and seasoning. Shape into 4 patties. In large nonstick skillet, brown patties over high heat. Remove and drain on paper towels.

Preheat oven to 375°. On lightly floured board, roll each biscuit into 6-inch circle; spread 4 circles with mustard and ketchup. Place a burger on each of these circles. Put pickle relish and a slice of onion on each burger. Moisten edge of biscuits and top with remaining biscuit circles. Press edges together with fork and prick tops. Bake on ungreased baking sheet 15–17 minutes. Makes 8.

Talk about expensive bread? Poilâne's (Paris) famous French sourdough bread sells for a whopping $19.50 a loaf.

In 1994, Diane Duyser of Florida noticed that the toasted sandwich she was eating appeared to contain an image of the Virgin Mary. She kept it for ten years (it never went moldy), before selling it to Canadian casino, Goldenpalace.com, in 2004 for $28,000.

Double or triple a recipe of sloppy joe mixture to freeze for taking to camps, tailgates, beach resorts, ski condos, etc. Pick up some buns, coleslaw, and chips, and you can feed a whole bunch of hungry people quite happily.

Sloppy Joe Phillies

5 slices bacon, chopped
¾ (12-ounce) package frozen seasoning blend
(chopped onion, celery, pepper)
1 (8-ounce) package sliced fresh mushrooms
2 pounds ground round
Salt and pepper to taste
1½ cups grated cheese of choice

Cook bacon until barely crisp; add seasoning blend and mushrooms. When lightly browned, add ground round; season to taste. Cook until brown. Stir in cheese until melted. Serve on toasted buns or rolls of choice. Serves 6–10.

Favorite Sloppy Joes

1 pound ground beef
2–3 stalks celery, chopped
1 small onion, chopped
1 (8-ounce) can tomato sauce
¼ cup ketchup
¼ cup barbecue sauce
1 tablespoon brown sugar
1 teaspoon dry mustard
1 tablespoon Worcestershire
1 tablespoon vinegar
Salt and pepper to taste
Toasted buns

Brown ground beef, celery, and onion in large skillet; drain. Stir in remaining ingredients, except buns. Simmer 15 minutes. Serve on toasted buns with french fries and coleslaw. Serves 4–6.

Editor's Extra: Make even easier by using frozen seasoning blend (chopped onion, celery, pepper) for veggies.

West Coast Turkey Focaccia Wedges (page156)

Craisin Carrot Tea Sandwiches (page 145)

Mini Crab Melts (page 163)

Black and Blue Sliders (page 184)

Milano Chicken Pitas (page 180)

Sandwich Cookie Chocolate Nut Bars (page 206)

Pecan Pie Minis (page 210)

Mousse Shots (page 212)

Dressed Up Hot Dogs

Bring on the chips!

1½ cups finely chopped onions
3 tablespoons butter, divided
4 hot dog buns
2 Ball Park franks, split lengthwise
1 cup shredded sharp Cheddar cheese
1 cup chopped tomatoes
Relish, ketchup, mustard to taste

Sauté onions in 1½ tablespoons butter in skillet. Toast buns and put onions on half of each on 4 paper plates. Sauté frank halves in remaining butter in skillet. Place on top of onions. Put cheese in skillet with heat off, just to soften; quickly put on each frank. Now top it off with tomatoes and condiments of choice. Serve open-face. (You probably need a knife and fork.) Makes 4.

Crescent Dogs

8 hot dogs
4 slices American cheese, cut into 6 strips
1 (8-ounce) can crescent rolls

Slit hot dogs to within ½ inch of ends; insert 3 strips cheese in each slit. Separate dough into triangles; wrap around each hot dog. Place on cookie sheet, cheese side up. Bake in 375° oven 12–15 minutes till golden brown. Makes 8.

On the 4th of July, 2009, Joey Chestnut won the 94th Annual Nathan's Hot Dog Eating contest, by consuming a new world record of 68 hot dogs and buns and winning his third consecutive title.

Sold round-the-world, Americans are by far the biggest consumers of hot dogs . . . over 20 billion a year, 7 billion of these between Memorial Day and Labor Day.

193

whether you call it a hot dog, frank-furter, frank, wiener, or wienie, these babies are as American as baseball and apple pie! They are sold on the street from wagons and carts, in convenience stores, fast food chains, and even casual dining restaurants . . . at least on the kid's menu. Ball parks feature them with the likes of Fenway Franks and Dodger Dogs. "Take me out to the ballgame . . . ."

Pizza Dogs

Kids love these!

4 hot dog buns
4 slices mozzarella cheese, halved
4 hot dogs
½ cup pizza sauce
Grated Parmesan

Open buns and place 2 cheese halves on bottom sides. Put hot dogs on top; spoon sauce over dogs. Sprinkle with Parmesan. Place all 8 open halves on broiler pan; broil till naked half is toasted and filled side is bubbly.

Editor's Extra: For S'getti Dogs—same as above except use spaghetti sauce.

Bacon-Wrapped Cheese Dogs

8 hot dogs
8 hot dog buns
8 slices Swiss or American cheese
8 bacon slices, cooked
½ cup diced sweet or red onion
Barbecue sauce to taste

Grill hot dogs; toast buns lightly. Wrap cheese around hot dog (or cut in strips to fit over top) and place in bun. Add a strip of bacon, then spoon a ribbon of barbecue sauce down dog; spoon onions on top. Close the dog and dive in!

The State of the Dog

some hot dogs have their own style:

NEW YORK CITY DOG
Add steamed onions and pale yellow mustard sauce

KANSAS CITY DOG
With sauerkraut and melted Swiss cheese on a sesame seed bun

CHICAGO DOGS
Topped with yellow mustard, relish, chopped onions, tomato slices, and celery salt on a poppyseed bun

BALTIMORE FRIZZLED
Split and deep-fried

CONEY ISLAND DOGS
Topped with mustard, onions, chili without beans

SOUTHERN SLAW DOGS
With coleslaw on top

TEX-MEX DOGS
Add salsa, jack cheese, and jalapeños

CORN DOGS
Corn-battered and deep-fried on a stick

PIGS IN A BLANKET
Wrapped in pastry or biscuit and baked

SONORANS
Bacon-wrapped with jalapeños

MICHIGAN RED HOTS
All-meat chili, onions

ITALIAN-STYLE
Fried with fried onion, peppers, potatoes

HALF SMOKES
Sausage with chili, onions

Beer Brats on the Grill

Not as fast . . . but extra fabulous!

4 fresh bratwurst
1 (12-ounce) can beer
1 medium onion, sliced
1 small red bell pepper, cut into thin strips
1 small green bell pepper, cut into thin strips
1 tablespoon vegetable oil
Salt and pepper to taste
4 subway sandwich rolls, split
Spicy brown mustard

Boil brats in beer one minute, then simmer uncovered 20–25 minutes or until bratwurst are no longer pink in center. Cool; drain and wrap in foil.

Combine vegetables on large sheet of heavy foil. Drizzle with oil and sprinkle generously with salt and pepper. Place another sheet of foil over vegetables; fold up edges to form a packet. Refrigerate up to 24 hours.

Cook packets on grill over medium coals 5–10 minutes till vegetables are tender, turning once. Place bratwurst on grill 10 minutes till heated through.

Grill rolls lightly during last 1–2 minutes of grilling. Serve brats in mustard-lined rolls topped with vegetables. Serves 4.

Seasonings

Cajun

Taco

Bay

Italian

Greek

Salad Supreme

All of these seasoning mixes were created so that you can add great flavor to dishes without your having to use multiple seasonings. Make a batch and share individual shakers with friends as little "happies." Not only is it fun to present the gift itself, but to know that this gift will keep on giving every time they use it.

K's Cajun Seasoning Mix

The very best seasoning mix there is . . . you will want to use it every time you cook.

1 (26-ounce) box salt
3 tablespoons black pepper
2 tablespoons garlic powder
1 teaspoon onion powder
1 teaspoon nutmeg
2 tablespoons dried parsley flakes
4 tablespoons cayenne pepper
2 tablespoons chili powder

Mix all in large bowl. Fill a shaker for daily use; store remainder in tightly covered container.

Best Taco Seasoning Mix

This amplifies southwestern soups and salads . . . choose your decibels!

1 tablespoon sea salt
1 tablespoon black pepper
4 tablespoons chili powder
1 teaspoon onion powder
1 teaspoon garlic powder
1 teaspoon crushed red pepper
2 teaspoons paprika
2 tablespoons ground cumin
1 teaspoon dried oregano

Mix all in a container with a tight lid. Two heaping tablespoonfuls equals a 1 1/4-ounce package of taco seasoning mix.

Best Bay Seasoning Mix

Excellent on seafood and chicken dishes.

1 cup salt
2 tablespoons ground bay leaves
1 tablespoon celery salt
1 teaspoon dry mustard
2 teaspoons black pepper
1 teaspoon paprika
¼ teaspoon ground cloves
¼ teaspoon ground nutmeg
½ teaspoon red pepper
½ teaspoon ground mace
½ teaspoon ground cardamom

Mix and store in airtight container. Makes about 1½ cups.

I keep a large container of seasoning mix with a small plastic funnel inside for easy shaker filling. If you do it quickly, you can avoid the temptation to sneeze!

Best Italian Seasoning Mix

Great on tomato-based dishes and any dish that yearns for a bit more Italian flavor.

2 tablespoons dried basil
3 tablespoons dried parsley
2 teaspoons garlic powder
2 teaspoons onion powder
1 tablespoon dried oregano
2 teaspoons dried thyme
1 teaspoon dried rosemary
1 teaspoon black pepper

Mix and store in container with tight lid. Makes about ½ cup.

Editor's Extra: Sprinkle with or offer a little Parmesan or Romano cheese as an ideal complement.

Use a tablespoon of any of these seasonings with 1/4 cup soft butter to spread on bread before baking . . . or with some olive oil and maybe a little parmesan in a saucer for dipping bread. Good on vegetables or pasta, too.

Best Greek Seasoning Mix

So good on fish and fowl dishes . . . great in soups.

1 cup salt
1 tablespoon garlic powder
2 teaspoons onion powder
1 tablespoon dried oregano
1 tablespoon dried thyme
2 teaspoons dried basil
2 tablespoons black pepper
½ teaspoon sugar
1 teaspoon cornstarch

Mix and store in container with tight lid. Makes about 1 ½ cups.

Best Salad Supreme

Add a little crunch as well as flavor to green and pasta salads.

2 tablespoons grated Romano cheese
1 ½ teaspoons sesame seed
½ teaspoon poppyseed
½ teaspoon celery seed
¼ teaspoon garlic powder
1 teaspoon paprika
¾ teaspoon salt
¼ teaspoon coarsely ground black pepper
⅛ teaspoon cayenne pepper

Combine all ingredients well. Pour into an empty spice bottle and label; store chilled. Makes ¼ cup.

Sweets

Cakes

Cookies

Candies

Pies

Desserts

Honeycomb Cake

It looks like a honeycomb on top, but it tastes like "the bee's knees"—which is to say, "The Best!"

2 cups milk
1 (3-ounce) box cook-and-serve vanilla pudding
1 (18¼-ounce) box yellow cake mix
1 (12-ounce) package butterscotch morsels

Boil milk with pudding in 3-quart pot. Stir in cake mix, then pour into greased 9x13-inch baking pan. Sprinkle butterscotch morsels evenly on top. Bake 30 minutes at 350°. Cool before serving.

Totally Awesome Cake

It simply IS!

1 (18¼-ounce) box German chocolate cake mix
1 (14-ounce) can sweetened condensed milk
1 (8-ounce) jar caramel topping
1 (8-ounce) carton Cool Whip
1 cup Heath bits

Bake cake per package directions in a greased and floured 9x13-inch pan. Poke holes in baked cake with handle of a wooden spoon. Pour condensed milk over all holes. Pour caramel topping over all. Spread Cool Whip on top; sprinkle with Heath bits. Refrigerate.

A Beautiful Strawberry Cake

4 eggs
1 cup cooking oil
1 (18¼-ounce) box yellow cake mix
1 (3-ounce) box strawberry gelatin
½ cup boiling water
1 (5-ounce) package frozen strawberries

Beat eggs in mixer bowl; mix in oil and cake mix. Partially dissolve strawberry gelatin in boiling water; add to batter. Pour into greased tube or Bundt pan; bake one hour at 325°.

Easy Lemon Tea Cookies

A soft bite of heaven.

1 (18¼-ounce) box lemon cake mix
1 egg, beaten
2 cups Cool Whip, thawed
½ cup powdered sugar, sifted

Combine cake mix, egg, and Cool Whip in a large bowl; mix well. Drop by teaspoon into powdered sugar; roll to coat. Place 1½ inches apart on a greased cookie sheet. Bake at 350° for 10–15 minutes. Makes 4 dozen.

Chocolate Coconut Macaroons

⅔ cup semisweet chocolate morsels
2 (3½-ounce) cans flaked coconut
1 (14-ounce) can sweetened condensed milk
1 cup chopped nuts
½ cup all-purpose flour

Microwave chocolate in 8-cup measure for 1½ minutes on HIGH. Stir and add remaining ingredients. Drop from teaspoon onto greased cookie sheet. Bake 20 minutes in 275° oven. Makes 2–3 dozen.

Persons in the United Kingdom, Russia, Spain, and France routinely offer tea cakes (cookies) at just about any type of formal tea. As tea rooms have become more popular in the United States, tea cakes are often part of the Americanized version of a high tea. Generally, tea cakes are coated with a thin layer of confectioners' sugar.

spraying the measuring cup with non-stick spray before filling it with peanut butter helps the peanut butter slide out more easily. You can also fill the measuring cup with hot, hot water, empty, then measure peanut butter . . . or honey or syrup or shortening.

Flaky Frogs

These will hop away quickly.

1 cup white corn syrup
1 cup brown sugar
1 cup crunchy peanut butter
Pinch of salt
3 cups Special K cereal

Boil corn syrup and sugar. Remove from heat; stir in peanut butter and salt till smooth. Fold in Special K; drop by teaspoon onto wax paper. Makes about 18.

Pecan Moons

A classic . . . pure and simple.

1 cup butter, softened
2¾ cups all-purpose flour
4 tablespoons powdered sugar
4 teaspoons vanilla
1 cup finely chopped pecans
1 tablespoon ice water

Mix all well with hands. Roll small pieces between hands into crescent moons. Place on ungreased cookie sheet 1 inch apart. Bake at 350° until light brown. Remove and roll in additional powdered sugar while still hot. Cool, then roll in powdered sugar again. Makes 3 dozen.

Mix and Bake Cream Cheese Cookies

It's all about taste. . . .

½ cup butter, softened
½ (8-ounce) package cream cheese, softened
1 cup sugar
1 cup all-purpose flour
½ cup chopped pecans
1 teaspoon vanilla

Mix butter and cream cheese; add sugar, flour, nuts, and vanilla. Teaspoon onto ungreased cookie sheets. Bake at 350° for 10–12 minutes or until edges are brown. Makes about 5 dozen.

Cheesecake Cookie Muffins

This has the easiest "crust" you'll ever make.

¾ cup sugar
2 (8-ounce) packages cream cheese, softened
2 eggs
1 teaspoon vanilla
24 chocolate or vanilla cream-filled cookies
1 (21-ounce) can cherry pie filling

Cream sugar and cream cheese. Add eggs and vanilla. Put 1 cookie in each cupcake liner. Put 2 tablespoons of mix on top. Bake at 375° for 15–20 minutes till set. Let cool; put 1 tablespoon pie filling on top. Refrigerate. Makes 24.

Archibald Query invented Marshmallow Fluff, (a special formula of marshmallow crème) in 1917 in his kitchen, and began selling it door-to-door. During World War I there were serious shortages of sugar, one of the basic ingredients. Query sold the rights to his recipe to candy makers H. Allen Durkee and Fred Mower for $500. Durkee-Mower still produces it by the original batch process.

Devilishly Delicious Squares

1 stick butter, melted
1 (18¼-ounce) box devil's food cake mix
¾ cup creamy peanut butter
1 (7½-ounce) jar marshmallow crème

Mix butter and cake mix. Reserve 1½ cups for top. Pat remaining mixture into ungreased 9x13-inch pan. Top with mixture of peanut butter and marshmallow crème; spread evenly. Crumble reserved cake mixture over that. Bake 20 minutes at 350°. Cool; cut into squares. Makes 36.

Sandwich Cookie Chocolate Nut Bars

A sweet "sandwich" indeed.

18 chocolate sandwich cookies, crushed
½ stick butter, melted
1 (14-ounce) can sweetened condensed milk
1 (12-ounce) package chocolate chips, divided
½ cup chopped cashews or pecans

Combine cookies with butter. Press into 9x9-inch greased pan. Heat milk and half of chips in saucepan just until melted. Spread evenly over cookie crust. Bake at 350° for 20 minutes. Sprinkle with remaining chips and nuts. Cool and cut into 12 squares. *(See full-color photograph in third insert following page 192.)*

Editor's Extra: Bake 15 minutes in a 9x13-inch pan for "fudgy-er" bars.

Easy Awesome Almond Brittle

2½ tablespoons butter
½ cup sugar
1 cup blanched whole almonds
1 teaspoon vanilla
¾ teaspoon salt

Cook butter, sugar, and almonds in heavy skillet on medium-high heat till golden brown, about 10 minutes. Stir in vanilla and pour onto sheet of heavy-duty foil, spreading thinly. Sprinkle with salt. Break when cool. Store air-tight.

Cracker Toffee

There is nobody who doesn't love this!

1 stack (or more) club crackers
1 cup butter
1 cup packed brown sugar
1 (12-ounce) package semisweet chocolate morsels

Preheat oven to 400°. Lay crackers to touch on all sides on a foil-lined cookie sheet. Stir butter and brown sugar over high heat constantly for 3 minutes till bubbly. Pour over crackers evenly. Bake about 6 minutes till golden, but not browned. Remove and let sit 2 minutes. Spread chocolate evenly over candy. Let harden, then break into pieces.

Hershey's Kisses® were introduced in 1907. While it's not known exactly how Kisses got their name, it is a popular theory that the candy was named for the sound or motion of the chocolate being deposited during the manufacturing process.

Hershey's makes more than 80 million Kisses per day. It takes 45 Kisses to equal 1 pound of chocolate.

Chocolate Kisses Pie

You'll always be proud to serve this make-ahead dessert.

1 (12-ounce) package Hershey's Kisses
¼ cup milk
1 (8-ounce) package cream cheese, cut
1 (12-ounce) carton Cool Whip
1 chocolate ready-made pie crust

Peel and melt Kisses over medium heat in milk. Add cream cheese and stir until melted. Remove from heat and stir in Cool Whip. Pour into crust. Refrigerate until set. Serves 6–8.

Heavenly Hawaiian Pie

Couldn't be easier! or more heavenly.

1 (14-ounce) can sweetened condensed milk
½ cup lemon juice
1 cup flaked coconut
1 cup chopped pecans
1 (8-ounce) can crushed pineapple, drained
1 (8-ounce) container Cool Whip, thawed
1 (9-inch) graham cracker pie shell

Mix all ingredients together and pour into pie shell. Chill and serve.

Chocolate Coffee Ice Cream Pie

A very cool dessert.

1 (8-ounce) chocolate almond bar
¼ cup coffee
1 (9-inch) graham cracker crust, baked
1 quart coffee ice cream, slightly softened
¼ cup Heath bits

Microwave chocolate bar with coffee 1 minute on HIGH; stir; heat additional time till melted. Spread over crust and cool. Fill with ice cream. Top with Heath bits; freeze. Remove 10 minutes before serving. Serves 6–8.

High-Five Peanut Butter Pie

1 (8-ounce) package cream cheese, softened
½ cup sugar
½ cup peanut butter
1 teaspoon vanilla
1 (12-ounce) carton Cool Whip, thawed
1 (9-inch) graham cracker crust
2 tablespoons chopped salted peanuts

Mix cream cheese with sugar. Add peanut butter and vanilla; beat well. Fold in Cool Whip. Pour into crust. Sprinkle with peanuts. Chill well. Serves 6–8.

Editor's Extra: Use real whipped cream for a richer taste.

Pecan Pie Minis

2 packages frozen mini fillo shells
1 1/4 cups chopped pecans
2 eggs, beaten
2/3 cup dark brown sugar
2/3 cup corn syrup
3 tablespoons butter, melted
1/2 teaspoon vanilla
Dash of salt

Place fillo shells into mini muffin pans. Divide pecans into each shell. Stir remaining ingredients together and spoon over pecans to 2/3 full. Bake 20–25 minutes at 350° till browned. Makes 24. *(See full-color photograph in third insert following page 192.)*

Editor's Extra: If you can't find fillo (phyllo) shells, you can use regular pie dough. Roll dough thinly. Cut small circles with floured biscuit cutter or glass. Press down into mini muffin pans and flare edges.

Pink Cloud Bing Cherry Pie

1 (14-ounce) can condensed milk
1 (16-ounce) can dark sweet cherries, drained
1/4 cup lemon juice
Several drops red food coloring
1 (8-ounce) carton Cool Whip
1 (9-inch) graham cracker crust, baked, cooled

Combine milk, cherries, juice, and food coloring. Fold in Cool Whip. Pour into graham cracker crust, chill, and serve. Serves 6–8.

A Little Chocolate Cherry Trifle

Not so big in size, but so delicious, you may have to double it next time!

1 (7x11-inch) pan fudge brownies
1 (6-pack) individual chocolate puddings
3 tablespoons coffee or coffee liqueur
½ (21-ounce) can cherry pie filling
1 (8-ounce) carton Cool Whip, thawed

Crumble brownies and place half in bottom of a 2-quart trifle bowl; drizzle with half the liqueur. Dot with half the cherry pie filling; layer with half the pudding, then half Cool Whip. Repeat layers. Garnish with chocolate curls, mini-chocolate morsels, or maraschino cherries.

Ice Cream Sandwich Dessert

6 ice cream sandwiches
⅔ (21-ounce) can cherry pie filling
1 (8-ounce) carton Cool Whip
½ (7-ounce) bottle chocolate shell

Lay 3 sandwiches on bottom of small casserole to fit. Pour ⅔ of pie filling over top; spoon half of whipped topping over this. Lay 3 more ice cream sandwiches on top; cover with remaining whipped topping. Drizzle chocolate shell over top. Garnish with dollops of more whipped cream and a spoon or two of cherry pie filling, if desired.

The earliest known use of the name trifle was for a thick cream flavored with sugar, ginger, and rosewater, the recipe for which was published in 1596 in a book called The Good Huswife's Jewell. It wasn't until sixty years later when milk was added and the custard was poured over alcohol-soaked bread.

Mousse Shots

You only need a few spoonfuls of this rich, delectable mousse to satisfy your chocolate craving. Have a shot!

1 ¼ cups chocolate morsels
1 tablespoon strong coffee
¾ cup scalded milk
1 egg, beaten
1 tablespoon liqueur (Grand Marnier, crème de menthe, sherry, dark rum, or amaretto)

Blend all in blender 90 seconds. Pour into 6–8 shot glasses (or liqueur glasses). Refrigerate till set. Garnish with whipped cream and a cherry, if desired. *(See full-color photograph in third insert following page 192.)*

Bread Pudding in a Flash

5–6 slices stale bread
2 cups milk
3–4 tablespoons butter
⅔ cup sugar
3 eggs, slightly beaten
1 teaspoon vanilla
½ teaspoon cinnamon
½ cup raisins

In microwave baking dish, soak torn bread in milk. Melt butter in 4-cup measure; add remaining ingredients. Pour over soaked bread, stirring only to distribute raisins. Microwave on ROAST (#7) for 11–14 minutes, until middle is no longer liquid.

Editor's Extra: This cooks beautifully in a glass ring. If you don't have one, put a custard cup upside down in center of round casserole, and put bread pudding mixture around it.

Index

ALMONDS:
Easy Awesome Almond Brittle 207
Fruit and Nut Slaw 87

APPLES:
Apple Cheese Sandwiches 146
Creamy Apple-Beet Salad 97
Honey Apple Coleslaw 89
Nutty Cranberry Apple Salad 96
Peanutty Apple Salad 97
Tangy Apple Nut Salad 98
Tropical Waldorf 96
Turkey Waldorf Salad 121
Apricot Vinaigrette 81

ASPARAGUS:
Ham and Asparagus Chowder 48
Tomato Basil Pasta Salad 109

AVOCADOS:
Avo-Cosmic Sandwich 162
Avocado-Mayo Dressing 137
Grapefruit and Avocado Salad 102
Light Taos Chicken Salad 115
Margarita Salad 115

BACON:
Bacon and Egg Sandwiches 150
Bacon Dressing 124
Bacon-Wrapped Cheese Dogs 194
BLT Salad 75
Burgundy Bacon Beef Stew 60
Quick Bean 'n Bacon Chowder 46
Ranch, Bacon, 'n Tato Salad 86
Wilted Greens 'n Bacon Salad 82
Bay Seasoning Mix, Best 199

BEANS: see also Chilis
Asian Chicken and Bean Salad 120
Cajun Bean and Chicken Soup 31
Cantastic Taco Bean Stew 61
Cheesy Black Bean Soup 19
Chili Bean Burgers 189
Classic Taco Ranch Soup 34
Greens, Beans, Carrots, and Things Soup 14
Hearty Bean and Beef Salad 123
Three Bean Chicken Chili 69
Porky Pig Black Bean Stew 61
Quick Bean 'n Bacon Chowder 46
Quick Chick Navy Bean Soup 31

Quick-To-Fix Burritos 182
Rainbow Three Bean Salad 94
Speedy Red Beans and Rice Soup 37
Succotash Salad 92
White Bean Soup 18

BEEF:
Beef Chilis:
Corny Chili 66
Hearty Home-Style Chili 65
Southwest Slow Cooker Chili 65

Beef Salads:
Fruit Salad over Grilled Steak 125
Hearty Bean and Beef Salad 123
Leafy Taco Salad 126
Mighty Meaty Chef's Salad 122
Sirloin Beef Salad 124
Steak Strip Meal Salad 123

Beef Sandwiches: see also Burgers
Avo-Cosmic Sandwich 162
Barbecue Brisket Sandwiches 169
Build-Your-Own Tacos 183
Corned Beef and Cabbage Sandwiches 166
Everybody Loves Meatball Subs 172
Hero Gyros 181
Macho Meatloaf Sandwich 166
Open-Face Roast Beef and Gravy Po-Boats 175
Open-Faced Reubens 165
Philly Cheesesteak Sandwich 167
Pizza Hoagies 174
Queso Wraps 182
Roast Po-Boys in a Packet 176
Steak 'n Mushroom Rolls 170
Stromboli-o-li Bread 168
Superfast Hoagies 174
Traditional Club Sandwich 155
Two-For-One Rib-Eye Sandwiches 169

Beef Soups:
Classic Taco Ranch Soup 34
Everything-But-The-Kitchen-Sink Soup 36
Mighty Meaty Meatball Soup 35
Pepe Meatball Soup 35
Speedy Chili–Soup 37
Traditional Vegetable-Beef Soup 12

Tri-Color Pepper Soup 36
Beef Stews:
Burgundy Bacon Beef Stew 60
Cantastic Taco Bean Stew 61
Cola Beef Stew 60
Easy Oven Stew 59
Good, Good Goulash 63
Hungarian Goulash 64
Mama's Old-Fashioned Stew 57
Slow Oven Stew 59
Two-Step Stew 58

BEETS:
An Un-beet-able Combo Salad 80
Borscht Made Easy 15
Creamy Apple-Beet Salad 97

BELL PEPPERS:
Cabbage Pepper Slaw 88
Cool and Ready Red Pepper Soup 71
Easy Roasted Red Pepper Soup 16
Pepper Snapper Soup 39
Spinach and Roasted Red Bell Pepper Salad 81
Tri-Color Pepper Soup 36

BISQUES:
A Dilly of a Salmon Bisque 45
Big Taste Tomato Basil Bisque 45
Crab Bisque the Easy Way 44
Lobsta Bisque 44
Minute Shrimp Bisque 43
Smooth and Silky Shrimp Bisque 43
Brats on the Grill, Beer 196
Bread Pudding in a Flash 212
Brittle, Easy Awesome Almond 207

BROCCOLI:
Broc & Chic Chowder 48
Broccoli Dressing 83
Secret Broccoli Soup 22
Traditional Broccoli Salad 83

BRUNCH SANDWICHES: see Tea Sandwiches

BURGERS:
Awesome Hamburgers 184
Biscuit Burgers 191
Black and Blue Sliders 184
Blue Cheese Burgers 186
Cajun Burgers 188
Cheese-Stuffed Burgers 185
Chili Bean Burgers 189
Favorite Sloppy Joes 192
Juicy French Dip Burgers 185
Mexican Cheeseburgers 187
Mushroom Hamburgers 186
No Guilt Turkey Burgers 190
Oriental Hamburgers 189

Parmigiana Venison Burgers 190
Pizza Burgers 188
Sloppy Joe Phillies 192
Supercalifragilistic Cheeseburgers 187
Veggie Cheeseburgers 191

CABBAGE: see also Coleslaw
Cabbage Dressing 88
Corned Beef and Cabbage Sandwiches 166
Mama's German Potato Salad 84
Ribbon Nest Pork Salad 122
Sweet and Sour Chicken Wraps 177
Cajun Burgers 188
Cajun Seasoning Mix, K's 198
CAKES:
A Beautiful Strawberry Cake 203
Honeycomb Cake 202
Totally Awesome Cake 202
Calzones, Easy Pepperoni 170
CANDIES:
Cracker Toffee 207
Easy Awesome Almond Brittle 207
CARROTS:
Cool Carrot Soup 70
Craisins Carrot Tea Sandwiches 145
Cranberry Carrot Salad 84
Greens, Beans, Carrots, and Things Soup 14
CHEESE:
Cheese Salads:
Blue Cheese or Roquefort Dressing 138
Blue Cheese Salad 77
Blue Cheese Vinaigrette 129
Chicken, Cherry, Cheese Salad 116
Ham 'n Cheese Rice Salad 110
Low-Fat Blue Cheese Dressing 138
Cheese Sandwiches:
Apple Cheese Sandwiches 146
Bacon-Wrapped Cheese Dogs 194
Baked Ham and Cheese Pizza Pockets 179
Ham & Cheese Bagels 150
Hot Cheese Sandwich in a Packet 159
Hot Chic 'n Cheese Packets 158

Hot Mini Ham & Swiss Buns 148
Kicky Grilled Cheese Sandwich 157
Peachy Cheese Deckers 147
Queso Wraps 182
Tupper's Favorite Pimento Cheese Sandwiches 145
Veggie & Cheese Muffuletta 151
Winning Grilled Cheese 157
Cheese Soups:
A Mighty Fine Cheddar Cheese Soup 23
Cheese with Beer Soup 23
Cheesy Black Bean Soup 19
Cheesy Corn & Crab Chowder 51
Dog and Cheese Chowder 53
Easy Cheesy Veggie Soup 12
Western Cheese Corn Soup 18
CHEESEBURGERS: see Burgers
CHERRIES:
A Little Chocolate Cherry Trifle 211
Black Cherry Salad 104
Cheesecake Cookie Muffins 205
Chicken, Cherry, Cheese Salad 116
Overnight Cherry Whip Salad 103
Pink Cloud Bing Cherry Pie 210
CHICKEN:
Chicken Chilis:
Blue Buffalo Chicken Chili 69
Three Bean Chicken Chili 69
White Chili in a Bread Bowl 68
Chicken Salads:
Asian Chicken and Bean Salad 120
Big Island Chicken Salad 117
Catalina Chicken Salad 113
Chicken, Cherry, Cheese Salad 116
Chicken Salad in Tomato Flowers 113
Chicken Salad Sandwiches 154
Fruity Chicken Salad 119
Greek Salad of the Gods 116
Light Taos Chicken Salad 115
Make-Ahead Chicken Penne Salad 108
Margarita Salad 115
Nutty Chicken Salad 114
Overnight Chicken Pasta Salad 107
Overnight Pepperoni Chicken Salad 118

Pretty-As-A-Picture Spinach Salad 78
Southwest Chicken Caesar Salad 118
Supreme Chicken Salad 119
Strawberry-Pecan Chicken Salad 114
Tall Tex Taco Salad 117
Chicken Sandwiches:
Biscuit Sandwiches 150
Buffalo Chicken on a Roll 161
Busy Mom's Hobo to Go 160
Chicken Canoes 159
Chicken Caesar Salad Wraps 177
Chicken Salad Sandwiches 154
Hot Chic 'n Cheese Packets 158
Mesquite Grilled Chicken on a Bun 161
Mighty Caesar Subs 172
Milano Chicken Pitas 180
Pocket Full of Nuggets 179
Queso Wraps 182
Sweet and Sour Chicken Wraps 177
Chicken Soups:
Broc & Chic Chowder 48
Cajun Bean and Chicken Soup 31
Chicken Noodle Veggie Soup Mix 10
Chicken Soup with Rivels 29
Cream of Chicken Corn Chowder 50
Creamy Chicken and Wild Rice Soup 28
Creamy Chicken Taco Soup 33
Easy Chicken and Crab Gumbo 54
In-A-Flash Tortilla Soup 32
Kicky Corn and Chicken Chowder 49
Quick Chick Navy Bean Soup 31
Sassy Chicken Salsa Soup 33
Short-Cut Chicken Noodle Soup 30
Slow-Cooker Gumbo 55
Southwest Chicken Stew 62
Tangy Chicken Soup 30

CHILIS:
Blue Buffalo Chicken Chili 69
Chunky Salsa Chili 67
Corny Chili 66
Hearty Home-Style Chili 65
Hot Chili for Two 66
Speedy Chili–Soup 37
Southwest Slow Cooker Chili 65
Three Bean Chicken Chili 69
White Chili in a Bread Bowl 68
Zesty Meatless Chili 67
CHILLED SOUPS: see Soups
CHOCOLATE:
A Little Chocolate Cherry Trifle 211
Chocolate Coconut Macaroons 203
Chocolate Coffee Ice Cream Pie 209
Chocolate Kisses Pie 208
Cracker Toffee 207
Devilishly Delicious Squares 206
Mousse Shots 212
Sandwich Cookie Chocolate Nut Bars 206
Totally Awesome Cake 202
CHOWDERS:
Ahoy Mate Oyster Chowder 53
Broc & Chic Chowder 48
Cheesy Corn & Crab Chowder 51
Cream of Chicken Corn Chowder 50
Creamy Crab Chowder 52
Dog and Cheese Chowder 53
Fast Potato and Ham Chowder 47
Ham and Asparagus Chowder 48
Hash Brown Oyster Chowder 52
Kicky Corn and Chicken Chowder 49
Loaded Baked Potato Chowder 47
Quick Bean 'n Bacon Chowder 46
Veggie-Tortellini Chowder 46
Coconut Macaroons, Chocolate 203
COLD CUTS: see Deli Meats
COLD SANDWICHES: see also Subs, Tea and Brunch Sandwiches
After Thanksgiving Sandwich 152
Chicken Salad Sandwiches 154
Duke of Windsor Sandwich 152

Lobster Salad Roll 153
Naka's Lettuce Sandwich 156
Open-Face Shrimp Sandwiches 153
Open-Face Salmon on Rye 154
Superfast Hoagies 174
Traditional Club Sandwich 155
Veggie & Cheese Muffuletta 151
Veggie Wedges 151
West Coast Focaccia Wedges 156
COLESLAW:
Cabbage Pepper Slaw 88
Easy Oriental Slaw 89
Fruit and Nut Slaw 87
Honey Apple Coleslaw 89
Mose's Just Right Coleslaw 87
Pineapple Coleslaw 88
Southwestern Salsa Coleslaw 173
COOKIES AND BARS:
Cheesecake Cookie Muffins 205
Chocolate Coconut Macaroons 203
Devilishly Delicious Squares 206
Easy Lemon Tea Cookies 203
Flaky Frogs 204
Mix and Bake Cream Cheese Cookies 205
Pecan Moons 204
Sandwich Cookie Chocolate Nut Bars 206
CORN:
Cheesy Corn & Crab Chowder 51
Corny Chili 66
Cream of Chicken Corn Chowder 50
Kicky Corn and Chicken Chowder 49
Roasted Corn Soup Topped with Crabmeat 17
Sea Scallops and Fried Corn Soup 40
Succotash Salad 92
Western Cheese Corn Soup 18
CRAB:
Cheesy Corn & Crab Chowder 51
Crab Bisque the Easy Way 44
Crab Louie Salad 127
Creamy Crab Chowder 52
Easy Chicken and Crab Gumbo 54
Mini Crab Melts 163
Open-Face Crab English Muffins 149

Roasted Corn Soup Topped with Crabmeat 17
West Indies Crab Salad 126
CRANBERRIES:
After Thanksgiving Sandwich 152
Biscuit Sandwiches 150
Chilly Cranberry Soup 72
Craisins Carrot Tea Sandwiches 145
Cranberry Carrot Salad 84
Cranberry Feta Green Salad 79
Nutty Cranberry Apple Salad 96
CUCUMBERS:
Cucumber Tea Sandwiches 144
Gotcha Gazpacho 70
Sea & Cuke Croissants 144

DELI MEATS:
Avo-Cosmic Sandwich 162
Mighty Meaty Chef's Salad 122
Monte Cristo Sandwiches 162
Superfast Hoagies 174
Traditional Club Sandwich 155
West Coast Focaccia Wedges 156
DESSERTS: see also Cakes, Candies, Cookies, Pies
A Little Chocolate Cherry Trifle 211
Bread Pudding in a Flash 212
Ice Cream Sandwich Dessert 211
Mousse Shots 212

EGGS:
Bacon and Egg Sandwiches 150
Egg Drop Soup 27
Extra Special Egg Salad 148
Kicked-Up-A-Notch Egg Salad 90

FISH: see also specific type of fish
Bayou Fish Soup 38
Capt'n's Choice Fish Sandwich 164
Pepper Snapper Soup 39
Ten-Minute Cioppino 38
FRUIT: see also specific fruit
   FRUIT SALADS: see also Gelatin Salads
Beautiful Watermelon Salad 95
Caribbean Mango Shrimp Salad 128
Celestial Salad 80

Classic Pineapple-Orange Salad 98
Creamy Apple-Beet Salad 97
Easy Ambrosia 99
Fruit and Nut Slaw 87
Fruit Salad over Grilled Steak 125
Fruit Salad with Cottage Cheese 99
Fruity Chicken Salad 119
Grapefruit and Avocado Salad 102
Honey Apple Coleslaw 89
Mixed Berry Salad 104
Nutty Cranberry Apple Salad 96
Overnight Cherry Whip Salad 103
Party Summer Salad 101
Peanutty Apple Salad 97
Pineapple Coleslaw 88
Rainbow Melon Salad 102
Shrimp 'n Melon Salad 128
Summer Fruit Salad 100
Tangy Apple Nut Salad 98
Tropical Waldorf 96
Turkey in the Orchard Salad 121
Whatevahyagot Fruit Salad 100
Fruit Sauce 99

 G

GELATIN SALADS:
Black Cherry Salad 104
Classic Pineapple-Orange Salad 98
Hello Jell-O Salad 106
Strawberry Pretzel Salad 105
Nutty Lime Jell-O Salad 106
GOULASHES:
Good, Good Goulash 63
Hungarian Goulash 64
Grapefruit and Avocado Salad 102
GREEK:
Best Greek Seasoning Mix 200
Greek Dressing 116
Greek Salad Dressing 140
Greek Salad of the Gods 116
GREEN SALADS:
An Un-beet-able Combo Salad 80
BLT Salad 75
Blue Cheese Salad 77
Celestial Salad 80
Classic Cobb Salad 74
Cranberry Feta Green Salad 79

Fabulous Fontina Salad 75
Mandarin Spinach Salad 81
Pretty-As-A-Picture Spinach Salad 78
Sassy Caesar Salad 82
Simply Italian Salad 76
Spinach and Roasted Red Bell Pepper Salad 81
Strawberry Brie Salad 79
The Best Romaine Salad 76
Touch of Tuscany Salad 77
Wilted Greens 'n Bacon Salad 82
Greens, Beans, Carrots, and Things Soup 14
GUMBOS:
Easy Chicken and Crab Gumbo 54
Quick Gumbo 56
Short-Cut Shrimp Gumbo 54
Slow-Cooker Gumbo 55

 H

HAM:
A Mighty Fine Cheddar Cheese Soup 23
Baked Ham and Cheese Pizza Pockets 179
Biscuit Sandwiches 150
Cuban Sandwich 167
Fast Potato and Ham Chowder 47
Ham & Cheese Bagels 150
Ham and Asparagus Chowder 48
Ham 'n Cheese Rice Salad 110
Hot Mini Ham & Swiss Buns 148
Hotty Toddy Ham Wraps 178
Mighty Meaty Chef's Salad 122
Monte Cristo Sandwiches 162
Porky Pig Black Bean Stew 61
Split Pea and Ham Soup 24
Superfast Hoagies 174
Traditional Club Sandwich 155
HAMBURGERS: see Burgers
HOT DOGS AND BRATS:
Bacon-Wrapped Cheese Dogs 194
Beer Brats on the Grill 196
Crescent Dogs 193
Dog and Cheese Chowder 53
Dressed Up Hot Dogs 193
Pizza Dogs 194
The State of the Dog 195
HOT SANDWICHES: see also Burgers, Hot Dogs, Pockets, Po-Boys, Subs, Wraps
Avo-Cosmic Sandwich 162

Barbecue Brisket Sandwiches 169
Buffalo Chicken on a Roll 161
Busy Mom's Hobo to Go 160
Capt'n's Choice Fish Sandwich 164
Chicken Canoes 159
Corned Beef and Cabbage Sandwiches 166
Cuban Sandwich 167
Easy Pepperoni Calzones 170
Griddle Pizza Sandwiches 171
Hawaiian Spam Bunwiches 164
Hot Cheese Sandwich in a Packet 159
Hot Chic 'n Cheese Packets 158
Kicky Grilled Cheese Sandwich 157
Macho Meatloaf Sandwich 166
Mesquite Grilled Chicken on a Bun 161
Mini Crab Melts 163
Monte Cristo Sandwiches 162
Open-Faced Reubens 165
Pizza in a Crescent 171
Steak 'n Mushroom Rolls 170
Stromboli-o-li Bread 168
Terrific Toasted Tuna Melts 163
Turkey Reubens 165
Two-For-One Rib-Eye Sandwiches 169
Winning Grilled Cheese 157

I

ICE CREAM:
Chocolate Coffee Ice Cream Pie 209
Ice Cream Sandwich Dessert 211
Italian Seasoning Mix, Best 199

L

LAMB:
Hero Gyros 181
Lemon Tea Cookies, Easy 203
LETTUCE: see also Green Salads
Naka's Lettuce Sandwich 156
Lime Jell-O Salad, Nutty 106
LOBSTER:
Lobsta Bisque 44
Lobster Salad Roll 153

217

 M

MANGOS:
Caribbean Mango Shrimp Salad 128
Party Summer Salad 101
Marinade, Maria's Garlic Tomato 133
Mayo My Way 141
Meatloaf Sandwich, Macho 166
MEATS: see Beef, Chicken, Deli Meats, Ham, Pork, Sausage, Turkey, Venison
MELONS: see also Watermelon
Party Summer Salad 101
Rainbow Melon Salad 102
Shrimp 'n Melon Salad 128
Mousse Shots 212
MUFFULETTAS:
Muffuletta Salad 90
Veggie & Cheese Muffuletta 151
MUSHROOMS:
A Mighty Good Mushroom Wrap 178
Fresh Cream of Mushroom Soup 20
Homemade Mushroom Soup 20
Mushroom Hamburgers 186
Steak 'n Mushroom Rolls 170
Turkey Mushroom Soup 21

 O

OLIVES:
Italian Summer Salad 91
Muffuletta Salad 90
Olive Nut Spreadwiches 147
Veggie & Cheese Muffuletta 151
ONIONS:
Tres Bien French Onion Soup 16
Vidalia Onion Vinaigrette 134
ORANGE:
Classic Pineapple-Orange Salad 98
Mandarin Spinach Salad 81
Mandarin Wild Rice Salad 112
Margarita Salad 115
OYSTERS:
Ahoy Mate Oyster Chowder 53
Dressed Oyster Po-Boys 175
Hash Brown Oyster Chowder 52

 P

PASTA:
Everything-But-The-Kitchen-Sink Soup 36
Make-Ahead Chicken Penne Salad 108
Mighty Meaty Meatball Soup 35
Overnight Chicken Pasta Salad 107
Pasta Garden Salad 109
Pepe Meatball Soup 35
Short-Cut Chicken Noodle Soup 30
Shrimp Pasta Salad 107
Tomato Basil Pasta Salad 109
Tortellini Sorento Soup 26
Veggie-Tortellini Chowder 46
PEACHES:
Chilled Peach Soup 71
Peach Dressing 121
Peachy Cheese Deckers 147
Peanut Butter Pie, High-Five 209
PEANUTS:
Peanutty Apple Salad 97
Quick-To-Fix-Peanut Soup 21
PEAS:
At-The-Ready Soup Mix 10
Jolly Good English Pea Salad 83
Split Pea and Ham Soup 24
Steamin' John Soup 19
PECANS:
Candied Cinnamon Pecans 129
Fruit and Nut Slaw 87
Nutty Lime Jell-O Salad 106
Olive Nut Spreadwiches 147
Pecan Moons 204
Pecan Pie Minis 210
Sandwich Cookie Chocolate Nut Bars 206
Strawberry-Pecan Chicken Salad 114
Tangy Apple Nut Salad 98
PEPPERONI:
Easy Pepperoni Calzones 170
Overnight Pepperoni Chicken Salad 118
Wrap Around the Pepperoni 177
PEPPERS: see Bell Peppers
PICNIC SALADS: see also Coleslaw, Potatoes, Tomatoes
Cranberry Carrot Salad 84
Jolly Good English Pea Salad 83
Kicked-Up-A-Notch Egg Salad 90
Marinated Veggie Salad 93
Muffuletta Salad 90

Rainbow Three Bean Salad 94
Succotash Salad 92
Traditional Broccoli Salad 83
PIES:
Chocolate Coffee Ice Cream Pie 209
Chocolate Kisses Pie 208
Heavenly Hawaiian Pie 208
High-Five Peanut Butter Pie 209
Pecan Pie Minis 210
Pink Cloud Bing Cherry Pie 210
PINEAPPLE:
Big Island Chicken Salad 117
Classic Pineapple-Orange Salad 98
Duke of Windsor Sandwich 152
Heavenly Hawaiian Pie 208
Hello Jell-O Salad 106
Pineapple Coleslaw 88
Pineapple Tuna Salad 132
Tropical Waldorf 96
PIZZA:
Baked Ham and Cheese Pizza Pockets 179
Easy Pepperoni Calzones 170
Griddle Pizza Sandwiches 171
Pizza Burgers 188
Pizza Dogs 194
Pizza Hoagies 174
Pizza in a Crescent 171
PO-BOYS:
Dressed Oyster Po-Boys 175
Open-Face Roast Beef and Gravy Po-Boats 175
Roast Po-Boys in a Packet 176
POCKETS:
Baked Ham and Cheese Pizza Pockets 179
Build-Your-Own Tacos 183
Milano Chicken Pitas 180
Pocket Full of Nuggets 179
PORK: see also Ham, Sausage
Chunky Salsa Chili 67
Cuban Sandwich 167
Hero Gyros 181
Juicy Pig Hoagies 173
Porky Pig Black Bean Stew 61
Ribbon Nest Pork Salad 122
POTATOES:
Potato Salads:
All American Potato Salad 86
Best on the Deck Potato Salad 85
Mama's German Potato Salad 84
Ranch, Bacon, 'n Tato Salad 86

Potato Soups:
Fast Potato and Ham Chowder 47
Hash Brown Oyster Chowder 52
Loaded Baked Potato Chowder 47
Potato Soup in a Jar 11
Vichyssoise 72
Pudding in a Flash, Bread 212

RASPBERRIES:
Raspberry Vinaigrette 135
Nutty Chicken Salad 114
RICE:
At-The-Ready Soup Mix 10
Creamy Chicken and Wild Rice Soup 28
Florida Rice Salad 110
Ham 'n Cheese Rice Salad 110
Mandarin Wild Rice Salad 112
Really Nice Rice Salad 111
Speedy Red Beans and Rice Soup 37
Steamin' John Soup 19
Tri-Color Pepper Soup 36
2-Mug Tortilla Soup Mix 11
Rivels, Chicken Soup with 29

SALAD DRESSINGS: *see also Vinaigrettes*
Asian Dressing 120
Avocado-Mayo Dressing 137
Bacon Dressing 124
Blender Basil Dressing 135
Blue Cheese or Roquefort Dressing 138
Broccoli Dressing 83
Brown Derby's Cobb Salad Dressing 133
Caesar Dressing 82
Celery Seed Dressing 136
Choice Salad Dressing 140
Citrus Dressing 128
Creamy Dressing 119
Creamy Green Yogurt Dressing 137
Deck Dressing 85
Dill Dressing 109
Fontina Dressing 75
Gingery Dressing 114
Honey-Thyme Dressing 108
Kangaroo Ranch Dressing 137

Kum-Back Salad Dressing 141
Louie Dressing 127
Low-Fat Blue Cheese Dressing 138
Maria's Garlic Tomato Marinade 133
Mayo My Way 141
Mustard Dressing 110
Orange Honey Mustard Dressing 123
Oriental Dressing 89
Peach Dressing 121
Poppyseed Dressing 79, 96
Russian Tea Room's Russian Dressing 142
Sensation Salad Dressing 139
Sesame Dressing 112
Simple Thousand Island Dressing 142
Splendid Honey Mustard Dressing 140
Summer Salad Dressing 101
Traditional Green Goddess Dressing 139
Watermelon Dressing 95
Zesty Dressing 92
SALADS: *see also Coleslaw, Green Salads, Fruit Salads, Gelatin Salads, Pasta, Picnic Salads, Potatoes, Rice*
Beef Salads:
Fruit Salad over Grilled Steak 125
Hearty Bean and Beef Salad 123
Leafy Taco Salad 126
Mighty Meaty Chef's Salad 122
Sirloin Beef Salad 124
Steak Strip Meal Salad 123
Chicken Salads:
Asian Chicken and Bean Salad 120
Big Island Chicken Salad 117
Catalina Chicken Salad 113
Chicken, Cherry, Cheese Salad 116
Chicken Salad in Tomato Flowers 113
Chicken Salad Sandwiches 154
Fruity Chicken Salad 119
Greek Salad of the Gods 116
Light Taos Chicken Salad 115
Make-Ahead Chicken Penne Salad 108
Margarita Salad 115
Nutty Chicken Salad 114

Overnight Chicken Pasta Salad 107
Overnight Pepperoni Chicken Salad 118
Pretty-As-A-Picture Spinach Salad 78
Southwest Chicken Caesar Salad 118
Strawberry-Pecan Chicken Salad 114
Supreme Chicken Salad 119
Tall Tex Taco Salad 117
Mighty Meaty Chef's Salad 122
Ribbon Nest Pork Salad 122
Seafood Salads:
Caribbean Mango Shrimp Salad 128
Crab Louie Salad 127
Fit-For-A-King Chopped Salad 129
Grilled Salmon Salad 130
Mose's Tuna Salad 131
Pineapple Tuna Salad 132
Sautéed Shrimp over Tender Greens 127
Shrimp 'n Melon Salad 128
Simon Says Sample Simple Salmon Salad 131
Tuna-Cone Salads 132
West Indies Crab Salad 126
Turkey in the Orchard Salad 121
Turkey Waldorf Salad 121
SALMON:
A Dilly of a Salmon Bisque 45
Grilled Salmon Salad 130
Open-Face Salmon on Rye 154
Simon Says Sample Simple Salmon Salad 131
SANDWICHES: *see also Burgers, Cold Sandwiches, Hot Dogs, Hot Sandwiches, Pockets, Subs, Po-Boys, Wraps*
Beef Sandwiches: *see also Burgers*
Avo-Cosmic Sandwich 162
Barbecue Brisket Sandwiches 169
Build-Your-Own Tacos 183
Corned Beef and Cabbage Sandwiches 166
Everybody Loves Meatball Subs 172

219

Hero Gyros 181
Macho Meatloaf Sandwich 166
Open-Face Roast Beef and
  Gravy Po-Boats 175
Open-Faced Reubens 165
Philly Cheesesteak Sandwich
  167
Pizza Hoagies 174
Queso Wraps 182
Roast Po-Boys in a Packet 176
Steak 'n Mushroom Rolls 170
Stromboli-o-li Bread 168
Traditional Club Sandwich 155
Two-For-One Rib-Eye
  Sandwiches 169
Chicken Sandwiches:
  Biscuit Sandwiches 150
  Buffalo Chicken on a Roll 161
  Busy Mom's Hobo to Go 160
  Chicken Canoes 159
  Chicken Caesar Salad Wraps
    177
  Chicken Salad Sandwiches 154
  Hot Chic 'n Cheese Packets 158
  Mesquite Grilled Chicken on a
    Bun 161
  Mighty Caesar Subs 172
  Milano Chicken Pitas 180
  Pocket Full of Nuggets 179
  Queso Wraps 182
  Sweet and Sour Chicken Wraps
    177
Seafood Sandwiches:
  Capt'n's Choice Fish Sandwich
    164
  Lobster Salad Roll 153
  Mini Crab Melts 163
  Open-Face Salmon on Rye 154
  Open-Face Shrimp Sandwiches
    153
  Terrific Toasted Tuna Melts 163
Vegetable Sandwiches:
  Veggie & Cheese Muffuletta 151
  Veggie Cheeseburgers 191
  Veggie Wedges 151
SAUCES:
  Butter-Mustard Sauce 176
  Fruit Sauce 99
  Tzatziki Sauce 181
SAUSAGE:
  Beer Brats on the Grill 196
  Hot Chili for Two 66

Pizza in a Crescent 171
Porky Pig Black Bean Stew 61
Quick Gumbo 56
Slow-Cooker Gumbo 55
Speedy Red Beans and Rice Soup
  37
Stromboli-o-li Bread 168
Scallops and Fried Corn Soup 40
SEAFOOD: see also Crab, Shrimp
Seafood Salads:
  Caribbean Mango Shrimp Salad
    128
  Crab Louie Salad 127
  Fit-For-A-King Chopped Salad
    129
  Grilled Salmon Salad 130
  Mose's Tuna Salad 131
  Pineapple Tuna Salad 132
  Sautéed Shrimp over Tender
    Greens 127
  Shrimp 'n Melon Salad 128
  Simon Says Sample Simple
    Salmon Salad 131
  Tuna-Cone Salads 132
  West Indies Crab Salad 126
Seafood Sandwiches:
  Capt'n's Choice Fish Sandwich
    164
  Lobster Salad Roll 153
  Mini Crab Melts 163
  Open-Face Salmon on Rye 154
  Open-Face Shrimp Sandwiches
    153
  Terrific Toasted Tuna Melts 163
Seafood Soups:
  A Dilly of a Salmon Bisque 45
  Ahoy Mate Oyster Chowder
    53
  Bayou Fish Soup 38
  Cheesy Corn & Crab Chowder
    51
  Crab Bisque the Easy Way 44
  Creamy Crab Chowder 52
  Easy Chicken and Crab Gumbo
    54
  Lobsta Bisque 44
  Mai-Thai Good Shrimp Soup 41
  Minute Shrimp Bisque 43
  Pepper Snapper Soup 39
  Quick Gumbo 56
  Sea Scallops and Fried Corn
    Soup 40
  Short-Cut Shrimp Gumbo 54
  Smooth and Silky Shrimp
    Bisque 43
  Spicy Shrimp Soup 42

Ten-Minute Cioppino 38
SEASONINGS:
  Best Bay Seasoning Mix 199
  Best Greek Seasoning Mix 200
  Best Italian Seasoning Mix 199
  Best Salad Supreme 200
  Best Taco Seasoning Mix 198
  K's Cajun Seasoning Mix 198
SHRIMP:
  Bayou Fish Soup 38
  Caribbean Mango Shrimp Salad
    128
  Fit-For-A-King Chopped Salad 129
  Mai-Thai Good Shrimp Soup 41
  Minute Shrimp Bisque 43
  Open-Face Shrimp Sandwiches
    153
  Quick Gumbo 56
  Sautéed Shrimp over Tender
    Greens 127
  Sea & Cuke Croissants 144
  Short-Cut Shrimp Gumbo 54
  Shrimp 'n Melon Salad 128
  Shrimp Pasta Salad 107
  Smooth and Silky Shrimp Bisque
    43
  Spicy Shrimp Soup 42
  Ten-Minute Cioppino 38
SLAW: see Coleslaw
SLOPPY JOES:
  Favorite Sloppy Joes 192
  Sloppy Joe Phillies 192
SOUPS: see also Bisques, Chilis,
    Chowders, Gumbos, Stews
  Beef Soups:
    Classic Taco Ranch Soup 34
    Everything-But-The-Kitchen-
      Sink Soup 36
    Mighty Meaty Meatball Soup 35
    Pepe Meatball Soup 35
    Speedy Chili–Soup 37
    Traditional Vegetable-Beef Soup
      12
    Tri-Color Pepper Soup 36
  Cheese Soups:
    A Mighty Fine Cheddar Cheese
      Soup 23
    Cheese with Beer Soup 23
    Cheesy Black Bean Soup 19
    Cheesy Corn & Crab Chowder
      51
    Dog and Cheese Chowder 53
    Easy Cheesy Veggie Soup 12
    Western Cheese Corn Soup 18
  Chicken Soups:
    Broc & Chic Chowder 48

Cajun Bean and Chicken Soup 31
Chicken Soup with Rivels 29
Cream of Chicken Corn Chowder 50
Creamy Chicken and Wild Rice Soup 28
Creamy Chicken Taco Soup 33
Easy Chicken and Crab Gumbo 54
In-A-Flash Tortilla Soup 32
Kicky Corn and Chicken Chowder 49
Quick Chick Navy Bean Soup 31
Sassy Chicken Salsa Soup 33
Short-Cut Chicken Noodle Soup 30
Slow-Cooker Gumbo 55
Southwest Chicken Stew 62
Tangy Chicken Soup 30
Chilled Soups
Chilled Peach Soup 71
Chilly Cranberry Soup 72
Cool and Ready Red Pepper Soup 71
Cool Carrot Soup 70
Gotcha Gazpacho 70
Vichyssoise 72
Egg Drop Soup 27
Seafood Soups:
A Dilly of a Salmon Bisque 45
Ahoy Mate Oyster Chowder 53
Bayou Fish Soup 38
Cheesy Corn & Crab Chowder 51
Crab Bisque the Easy Way 44
Creamy Crab Chowder 52
Easy Chicken and Crab Gumbo 54
Lobsta Bisque 44
Mai-Thai Good Shrimp Soup 41
Minute Shrimp Bisque 43
Pepper Snapper Soup 39
Quick Gumbo 56
Sea Scallops and Fried Corn Soup 40
Short-Cut Shrimp Gumbo 54
Smooth and Silky Shrimp Bisque 43
Spicy Shrimp Soup 42
Ten-Minute Cioppino 38
Soup à la Tortilla 32
Soup Mixes:
At-The-Ready Soup Mix 10

Chicken Noodle Veggie Soup Mix 10
Potato Soup in a Jar 11
2-Mug Tortilla Soup Mix 11
Speedy Red Beans and Rice Soup 37
Turkey Mushroom Soup 21
Vegetable Soups:
A Mighty Fine Cheddar Cheese Soup 23
Big Taste Tomato Basil Bisque 45
Borscht Made Easy 15
Cheese with Beer Soup 23
Cheesy Black Bean Soup 19
Easy Cheesy Veggie Soup 12
Easy Roasted Red Pepper Soup 16
18 Karat Gold Italian Soup 15
Fresh Cream of Mushroom Soup 20
Greens, Beans, Carrots and Things Soup 14
Homemade Mushroom Soup 20
Quick & Thick Tomato Soup 25
Quick-To-Fix-Peanut Soup 21
Roasted Corn Soup Topped with Crabmeat 17
Roasted Vegetable Soup 13
Secret Broccoli Soup 22
Split Pea and Ham Soup 24
Steamin' John Soup 19
Suavy Sweet Potato Soup 24
The Real Deal Basil and Tomato Soup 25
Tortellini Sorento Soup 26
Touch of Curry Tomato Soup 26
Traditional Vegetable-Beef Soup 12
Tres Bien French Onion Soup 16
Turkey Mushroom Soup 21
Veggie-Tortellini Chowder 46
Western Cheese Corn Soup 18
White Bean Soup 18
Zesty Meatless Chili 67
Spam Bunwiches, Hawaiian 164
SPINACH:
Big Island Chicken Salad 117
Mandarin Spinach Salad 81
Pretty-As-A-Picture Spinach Salad 78
Spinach and Roasted Red Bell Pepper Salad 81

Tortellini Sorento Soup 26
Touch of Tuscany Salad 77
Wilted Greens 'n Bacon Salad 82
STEAK:
Fruit Salad over Grilled Steak 125
Sirloin Beef Salad 124
Steak 'n Mushroom Rolls 170
Steak Strip Meal Salad 123
Two-For-One Rib-Eye Sandwiches 169
STEWS:
Burgundy Bacon Beef Stew 60
Cantastic Taco Bean Stew 61
Cola Beef Stew 60
Easy Oven Stew 59
Good, Good Goulash 63
Hungarian Goulash 64
Mama's Old-Fashioned Stew 57
Porky Pig Black Bean Stew 61
Slow Oven Stew 59
Southwest Chicken Stew 62
Two-Step Stew 58
STRAWBERRIES:
A Beautiful Strawberry Cake 203
A Honey of a Strawberry Sandwich 146
Pretty-As-A-Picture Spinach Salad 78
Strawberry Brie Salad 79
Strawberry Dressing 78
Strawberry Pretzel Salad 105
Strawberry-Pecan Chicken Salad 114
SUBS:
Everybody Loves Meatball Subs 172
Juicy Pig Hoagies 173
Mighty Caesar Subs 172
Pizza Hoagies 174
Superfast Hoagies 174
Sweet Potato Soup, Suavy 24
SWEETS: *see Cakes, Candies, Cookies, Desserts, Pies*

TACO:
Best Taco Seasoning Mix 198
Build-Your-Own Tacos 183
Cantastic Taco Bean Stew 61
Classic Taco Ranch Soup 34
Creamy Chicken Taco Soup 33

Leafy Taco Salad 126
Tall Tex Taco Salad 117
TEA SANDWICHES:
A Honey of a Strawberry
Sandwich 146
Apple Cheese Sandwiches 146
Bacon and Egg Sandwiches 150
Biscuit Sandwiches 150
Craisins Carrot Tea Sandwiches
145
Cucumber Tea Sandwiches 144
Extra Special Egg Salad 148
Ham & Cheese Bagels 150
Hot Mini Ham & Swiss Buns 148
Olive Nut Spreadwiches 147
Open-Face Crab English Muffins
149
Peachy Cheese Deckers 147
Sea & Cuke Croissants 144
Tupper's Favorite Pimento Cheese
Sandwiches 145
Toffee, Cracker 207
TOMATOES:
Basil Trayed Tomatoes 91
Big Taste Tomato Basil Bisque 45
Chicken Salad in Tomato Flowers
113
Colorful Summertime Salad 93
Gotcha Gazpacho 70
Italian Summer Salad 91
Maria's Garlic Tomato Marinade
133
Quick & Thick Tomato Soup 25
Summertime Tomato &
Watermelon Salad 94
Sun-Dried Tomato Vinaigrette 135
Ten-Minute Cioppino 38
The Real Deal Basil and Tomato
Soup 25
Tomato Basil Pasta Salad 109
Touch of Curry Tomato Soup 26
Trifle, A Little Chocolate Cherry 211
TORTELLINI: see Pasta
TUNA:
Mose's Tuna Salad 131
Pineapple Tuna Salad 132
Terrific Toasted Tuna Melts 163
Tuna-Cone Salads 132

TURKEY:
After Thanksgiving Sandwich 152
Avo-Cosmic Sandwich 162
Biscuit Sandwiches 150
Duke of Windsor Sandwich 152
No Guilt Turkey Burgers 190
Monte Cristo Sandwiches 162
Superfast Hoagies 174
Traditional Club Sandwich 155
Turkey in the Orchard Salad 121
Turkey Mushroom Soup 21
Turkey Reubens 165
Turkey Waldorf Salad 121
West Coast Focaccia Wedges 15

VEGETABLES: see also Green
Salads, specific vegetable
Chicken Noodle Veggie Soup
Mix 10
Marinated Veggie Salad 93
Pasta Garden Salad 109
Vegetable Sandwiches:
Veggie & Cheese Muffuletta 151
Veggie Cheeseburgers 191
Veggie Wedges 151
Vegetable Soups:
A Mighty Fine Cheddar Cheese
Soup 23
Big Taste Tomato Basil Bisque
45
Borscht Made Easy 15
Cheese with Beer Soup 23
Cheesy Black Bean Soup 19
Easy Cheesy Veggie Soup 12
Easy Roasted Red Pepper Soup
16
18 Karat Gold Italian Soup 15
Fresh Cream of Mushroom
Soup 20
Gotcha Gazpacho 70
Greens, Beans, Carrots and
Things Soup 14
Homemade Mushroom Soup
20
Quick & Thick Tomato Soup 25
Quick-To-Fix-Peanut Soup 21
Roasted Corn Soup Topped
with Crabmeat 17
Roasted Vegetable Soup 13
Secret Broccoli Soup 22
Split Pea and Ham Soup 24
Steamin' John Soup 19
Suavy Sweet Potato Soup 24

The Real Deal Basil and Tomato
Soup 25
Tortellini Sorento Soup 26
Touch of Curry Tomato Soup 26
Traditional Vegetable-Beef Soup
12
Tres Bien French Onion Soup
16
Turkey Mushroom Soup 21
Veggie-Tortellini Chowder 46
Western Cheese Corn Soup 18
White Bean Soup 18
Zesty Meatless Chili 67
Venison Burgers, Parmigiana 190
VINAIGRETTES:
Apricot Vinaigrette 81
Blue Cheese Vinaigrette 129
Cabbage Dressing 88
Celestial Dressing 80
Dijon Vinaigrette 130
Fontina Dressing 75
Greek Dressing 116
Greek Salad Dressing 140
Light Balsamic Vinaigrette 134
Poppyseed Vinaigrette 136
Rainbow Vinaigrette 102
Raspberry Vinaigrette 135
Strawberry Dressing 78
Sun-Dried Tomato Vinaigrette 135
Tall Tex Dressing 117
Tuscany Dressing 77
Vidalia Onion Vinaigrette 134

WALNUTS:
Nutty Chicken Salad 114
Nutty Cranberry Apple Salad 96
Tangy Apple Nut Salad 98
WATERMELON:
Beautiful Watermelon Salad 95
Summertime Tomato &
Watermelon Salad 94
WRAPS:
A Mighty Good Mushroom Wrap
178
Chicken Caesar Salad Wraps 177
Hero Gyros 181
Hotty Toddy Ham Wraps 178
Queso Wraps 182
Quick-To-Fix Burritos 182
Sweet and Sour Chicken Wraps 177
Wrap Around the Pepperoni 177